THE MAN WHO KEEPS GOING TO JAIL

THE MAN WHO KEEPS GOING TO JAIL

JOHN R. ERWIN

David C. Cook Publishing Co.

ELGIN, ILLINOIS—WESTON, ONTARIO
FULLERTON, CALIFORNIA

Published by David C. Cook Publishing Co., Elgin, IL 60120
Edited by Ronald Wilson and Dean Merrill
Cover and inside photos of PACE by Bob McCullough
Printed in the United States of America

ISBN 0-89191-107-3
LC 77-088124

With love to

Earline and Herschner Coats
(Mom and Dad)

and
our dear children, Vance, Gregg, and Gayle,
who ate a lot of TV dinners
so this book could be written

Be as mindful of prisoners as if you were sharing their imprisonment, and of the ill-treated as of yourselves, for you may yet suffer as they do.

Hebrews 13:3, New American Bible

CONTENTS

FOREWORD

This account of the Reverend John R. Erwin's formative years and his career at Cook County Jail, including his dreams and their realization in PACE Institute, is one of the most inspiring stories I have ever known.

Because I had a small part in the formative stages of PACE Institute and because of my great affection and deep respect for John Erwin, I am delighted to present this foreword to *The Man Who Keeps Going to Jail.*

In my years of public life, I have met and known and worked with many people. Most of them are honest and decent—dedicated to doing a job of performing a service for the government or their community. However, one man stands out above all others as the most essentially good man I have ever known, and that is John Erwin. He literally lives the teachings of his religion.

John Erwin's successes with PACE Institute and what is being done for the inmates at Cook County Jail are now nationally recognized. The many expressions of interest from around the country are very heartening. It may be that there is a new day coming for those who get into trouble with the law and must serve time in one of our institutions. If this does come to pass, one man, John Erwin, deserves the credit for lighting a candle rather than cursing the darkness.

RICHARD B. OGILVIE
Former Governor of Illinois

11

PREFACE

For years people have said, "You should write a book."
(We hope they will still feel that way after reading it.)
Then publishers and writers began to urge us. When our
friend Cathy Davis of Cook Publishing Company
brought acquisitions editor Ron Wilson to the jail for a
visit, Ron persisted until we signed a contract in February, 1977, making '77 for us "the Year of the Book."
After countless hours of work, visits to former homes,
and long interviews with people in our past, we now look
at every book with deep respect and appreciation.

Special thanks to Sue Hickman and Willie Carter for
helping with the manuscript typing and refusing any
pay. And to editors Ron Wilson and Dean Merrill, thanks
for your skills and desire to make this the best book you
possibly could.

Above all, Dell and I thank the One who changed my
life so drastically at the age of twenty-two, healing the
wounds of my past and using them to better equip me for
my mission in life. He literally fulfilled a promise made in
Joel 2:25, "And I will restore to you the years that the
locust hath eaten. . . ."

It is our prayer that this book will promote a better
understanding for troubled people and motivate involvement in rehabilitation by love. We also trust our
story will cause you to join us in our life's verse, engraved
inside our wedding bands: "O magnify the Lord with me,
and let us exalt his name together" (Ps. 34:3).

WHY DON
CAN'T READ

ONE

WHEN SCANDAL BROKE OVER the old Cook County Jail in Chicago in the 1920s, a new $7.5 million court and jail complex was built. Those were the lusty Prohibition days of Big Bill Thompson and Al Capone and 200 gang killings in four years.

Anton J. Cermak, later a powerful mayor of Chicago, was then president of the county board, and when the jail opened they called it "Cermak's Folly." It had no heat and only partial plumbing. It was an outdated, Bastille-type maximum security prison, overcrowded from the first day, when 1,341 prisoners moved into a building built to house 1,300. From that time the reputation of Cook County Jail grew and spread around the world, deservedly or not, as a scandalous institution.

I first visited there as a Bible school student in 1954, and three years later became a chaplain. I knew little nor cared much about the thirty years of escapes, violence, graft, and overcrowding. I knew only that I wanted to use

17

what ability or gifts I had to help the 2,000 or so unfortunate men inside.

Each day I drove to the gray stone building at 26th and California and knocked on the armor-plated door. The guard peered through the hole, opened the door, checked my pass, and I went to work. For the first two years I stood on one side of a steel partition in the visitors' cages shouting spiritual counsel to the men on the other side. On Sundays, with volunteers from nearby churches, we entered the tiers of cells and held services for any prisoner who wanted to turn in our direction.

Finally the warden gave me office space in the basement. It was another step forward when they assigned me an inmate as a clerk, and I felt I had made real progress when they allowed me to begin a Wednesday night Bible study.

Even under the best conditions, however, jail work is slow. I had seen an occasional inmate go out and walk the straight and narrow path, but often I had watched men try to turn their lives around, only to end up again in the same jail, victims of their pasts, their environments, and their own natures.

One Wednesday evening in the fall of 1967, I hurried back to my office after the Bible study to check the list of attendants. In jail you routinely check and double-check, comparing one list against another.

I asked my clerk Don to read one list while I checked off the names on the other. I had a church meeting later in the evening and wanted to leave as soon as possible. With the list in hand and pen poised, I waited. But Don just sat there.

Growing impatient, I urged, "Don, let's hurry. Read!"

Still he sat there, his head down, his mouth twitching as if to say something.

Suddenly, it hit me like an explosion.

"Don," I asked quietly, "you can't read, can you?"

His embarrassment was too painful to watch as he answered, "No, Rev, I can't read a word."

I was stunned. Don was a well-mannered, conscientious young man who appeared articulate and educated, and he had done my clerical work efficiently for months. He had first been assigned to clean the chapel, and when my previous clerk was released, the jail officials had let Don take his place. (Later I learned that the Catholic chaplain's clerk had done his typing while Don did other jobs for him.)

As he returned to his cell, I sat there thinking about him and thousands like him. Twenty years old, Don had grown up on the South Side of Chicago, attended school, but never learned to read or write. He was a friendly, cheerful guy who had run with the Vice Lords on Chicago's West Side; they had nicknamed him Eagle. At home his mother berated him, called him dumb, the black sheep of the family. So did the teachers who told him he'd never learn. But the gang respected him, so Don, handsome and well built, found a home on the street until he landed in Cook County Jail. He had been in and out several times before he came to me.

As I drove home, I couldn't get Don off my mind. Something about him was dredging up the remembrances of my own past . . . a fifteen-year-old boy standing before a judge in an Indiana court and hearing him tell me, "You'll spend the rest of your life in institutions." I knew the long, downward spiral Don was following. I was again submerged in the defeat, the helplessness, the feeling of being a perpetual loser. I'd been there once.

AUNT ALICE AND UNCLE FRANK

TWO

As THE THIRTEENTH CHILD born to Vilas and Pearl Erwin, I was hardly a welcome addition. We lived in central Indiana during the Depression, supported mostly by the Marion County Department of Public Aid. The only job I ever knew my father had was with Roosevelt's WPA, which I was told, meant "We Poke Along."

I was six and in the hospital with complications from measles when an older sister visited me with the news that "Daddy has gone up above." I had no idea what that meant until I got home and realized I would never see him again. He had died of pneumonia.

A few months after that, my mother called together her three youngest—Joan, who was eight, myself, and five-year-old Louise—and told us we'd be going on a vacation. "I have a bad heart," she explained, "and I can't care for you. You'll be going out in the country to a place

THE MAN WHO KEEPS GOING TO JAIL

with lots of green grass and animals and some real fine folks, and one day I'll come get you."

As the social worker arrived and loaded our luggage, Louise got excited. She had never been on a vacation before. Joan was silent, however, as we drove away, and her silence said more than words could. I began to cry.

The drive to Tilden, Indiana, took more than an hour, but the car finally bumped over some railroad tracks and stopped near a cluster of farmhouses and a general store. I looked out apprehensively as a small, frail-looking woman adjusting a hairpin at the back of a gray bun came out to meet us.

"Y'all come in and make yourselves t' home."

Then she called, "Frank. The kids is here."

The man who came out of the blacksmith's shed next to the house looked like Paul Bunyan to me. He was huge with great sinewy arms. I had never seen such a face, covered with purplish, broken veins.

Our belongings were brought into the living room, and soon the social worker left. There was an awkward silence. Finally Joan asked, "What should we call you?"

"Why, just call us Aunt Alice and Uncle Frank," the woman replied. *Uncle* and *aunt* sounded friendly enough, but the words were hollow.

They led us around the house, showing us the room where I would sleep, the room that Joan and Louise would share. It seemed so unnatural to be in this place; I felt cold and alone. I was dwarfed by the gigantic Uncle Frank, who had little to say. The fear of the unknown pounded through my chest.

We settled into the routine of the household that summer, and in the fall I started first grade. We all had chores—dusting, sweeping, washing dishes, emptying slop jars, milking. I didn't mind the work, but things began to happen that I didn't understand.

Late one afternoon I walked into a semidarkened room, dimly lit by a flickering kerosene lamp, and saw two figures huddled together—Uncle Frank with Joan on his lap. Startled, Uncle Frank screamed, "Get outta here, boy! And don't come back in this house till you're called!"

After that I would often see Uncle Frank and Joan together, and in my six-year-old mind I knew something strange was going on. Whenever Aunt Alice found them, she would chase Joan out. The once meek, grandmotherly lady would rant and rage, and I was sure something was very wrong about this place.

One day when Aunt Alice went to visit a neighbor, Uncle Frank ordered Louise and me outside, then called Joan into the kitchen, and closed the door. Quietly Louise and I sneaked back into the house. The door into the kitchen had glass panes covered with frosted paper, but we could see the silhouettes of Uncle Frank and Joan kissing and touching each other. Giggling at this strange sight, we tiptoed outside.

In a few minutes, Aunt Alice returned and went into the house. Louise and I, sensing excitement, ran around to the kitchen window, found a block of wood, and pulled ourselves up to peer through.

Aunt Alice's shriek split the air. "You little whore!" Then a loud smack.

Louise huddled close to me as we heard Joan beg, "Please, stop." Aunt Alice knocked her to the floor.

Uncle Frank had fled the room, but his wife, now enraged, continued the attack. She grabbed Joan between the legs as she screamed, "I'll teach you to leave my husband alone, you no-good welfare brat!" Joan curled into a ball and lay sobbing while Aunt Alice kicked her again and again.

The harvesting of crops and preparation for winter

helped to take our minds off some of our fears that fall of 1937. We hulled hundreds of walnuts, picked persimmons, and canned vegetables, along with our regular chores. But by spring, I began wondering when our "vacation" would end. We had already been there nine months without a word from mother. And Joan was not alone in drawing the wrath of these strange foster parents. Uncle Frank had a thick razor strap that he used on my legs, sometimes until they bled.

One of my chores was to milk the cow before breakfast. I was always joined in the task by Jack, the three-legged dog. Somehow he fit into the place. Even the cow was odd—she had only two teats, and if I hadn't been told that this was a birth defect, I would have thought Aunt Alice or Uncle Frank jerked the others off in a fit of rage. One morning as I was about to put away the milking stool, the cow lifted her foot and plopped it in the pail. Slowly trudging back to the house, I watched the debris swimming in the milk and wondered which one would punish me.

This time Aunt Alice did the honors. I knew better than to cry, however. When I did she'd tell me, "Shut up or I'll throw salt in the wounds."

Soon Uncle Frank turned his sexual attentions to Louise as well, driving Aunt Alice to tears. Since they carefully censored all the letters we wrote, we couldn't tell anyone on the outside. Every day, it seemed, at least one of us got beaten for something.

Then came the long-awaited day.

One morning after breakfast Aunt Alice announced, "Your mother is coming for a visit tomorrow, and it's about time. That woman ought to be tarred and feathered for puttin' you kids out on welfare. Her heart ain't that bad."

We hardly noticed her gibe—we'd heard it many times

before, anyway. I just knew our "vacation" was about over. I gathered everything I owned so it could be quickly packed, and for the first time in months I began to feel at ease.

When mom arrived, she hugged us, and we sat down excitedly to hear what she had to say. The only trouble was, Aunt Alice remained in the room with us. Mom said nothing about a change for us. Instead, she and Aunt Alice carried on about crops, canning, and recipes for persimmon pudding.

Finally, during a lull in the conversation I blurted out, "When are we going home, mama?"

"Oh, you kids can't go home with me. I'm still not well enough to take care of you. I'll come back when I can. My, you do look healthy with those rosy cheeks." She pinched them.

We sat there, three silent knots, feeling as though the bottom of the world had dropped. I wanted to yell, *You have to take us! This place is hell!* But my tongue was frozen.

If a mother can't love her own child, who can? I wondered. If I'm not worthy of my mother's love, am I worthy of anything? With bitterness and anger I fled to the one private place I had found, the back of the barn, and sobbed. I had lost all hope, and I knew we'd never get out of this miserable place.

I wonder now how we did survive those four years. School was as much an ordeal as home. With the snap of Frank's razor strap in our ears and outdated clothes on our backs, we started each school day defeated. The social worker bought our clothes at one particular low-cost store and always reminded us that they belonged to the taxpayers. Aunt Alice allowed us a clean set of clothes only once a week, on Wednesdays. If we got them dirty, we still had to wear them all week.

We were not allowed to take part in any school social

activities, and I never developed any sports ability. My grades were poor, and so it's no wonder I hated most of the hours spent in school. The evidences of my failure were on all sides.

Finally one night in the spring of 1941, my sleep was interrupted by piercing screams. I bolted upright. Pushing aside the curtain that separated my room from the living room, I gazed with horror at the sight of my naked sisters being chased around the heating stove by Aunt Alice, who wielded two iron pokers in her upraised hands. "I told you to leave my husband alone!" she shrieked. "I'll kill both of you ------!"

At that moment, Uncle Frank tore into the room and managed to wrest the pokers from his hysterical wife. Shoving them at me, he ordered, "Here—hide 'em." I buried them in my bed and then crawled under the quilts, shaking and sobbing.

We were all going to be killed. I knew it.

Joan, Louise and I now decided to take matters into our own hands. At school we told the teachers about the way our foster parents treated us, but no one believed us. "These welfare kids. They're such liars," we heard them say. "Probably illegitimate. Always misfits." We talked to our Sunday school teachers, and came up against the same disbelief.

Undaunted, we marched to the house next door one day and spilled the story to Mrs. Phillips. Louise and Joan told of Uncle Frank's abuse, and I told about the beatings. When we were through, Mrs. Phillips chided, "You ought to be ashamed of yourselves. You welfare kids are all alike. Why, Frank and Alice are the finest people around! Now git on home."

But one evening shortly after that, Mrs. Phillips came over to our place on an errand, and Aunt Alice was away. Through the partially drawn shade she saw a shocking sight—a naked twelve-year-old girl on the lap of a naked man.

In a few days we were on our way to a new home.

We tried to shut from our minds the four years of sexual abuse and beatings, but even at age ten I knew the sores went much deeper than the red welts on my legs.

ONE TOUGH KID

THREE

I SPENT THE NEXT World War II years going in and out of foster homes like they had revolving doors. In the process I left behind the wide-eyed trusting boy on a "vacation" in the country for the scrappy take-care-of-myself-to-survive kid, dreaming by day and crying at night for someone, just someone, who would love me.

While Joan was sent to a separate foster home, Louise and I went to live with a Mrs. Meyers, a sturdily built German woman with a thick accent who ran a farm with the help of her married son. She already had one welfare kid there, David, a little older, bigger, and stronger than I, who took every opportunity to let me know he was better as well. When we picked tomatoes, David sneered, "Your basket isn't even full yet and I'm on my second one." When we milked the thirty Holsteins each morning, David proved he could do it faster. I met the challenge by shoving or tripping or punching him, and we fought on every acre of the farm.

Certainly Mrs. Meyers treated us fairly, even when Louise and I once declared we had worked enough and defiantly went on strike high in a maple tree. Frustrated, Mrs. Meyers began to throw rocks to get us to come down, and Louise and I finally decided we'd better cooperate with the rock thrower. Even then, however, we knew there'd be no beating.

Louise and David now seemed to be my real problem. They fought as much as David and I did, and I thought it was my duty to protect my little sister. Soon I resented her, though, imagining that she had also caused problems for me at our first foster home.

One afternoon after school Mrs. Meyers handed me a letter from my mother. It had been months since I'd heard from her. Now at last I had something to replace the mental tapes I kept hearing of Aunt Alice saying, "Your mother ought to be tarred and feathered. She could have kept you if she wanted. . . ." Hiding any feelings, I took the letter to my room and opened it.

Dear John,

How are you? I hope you're liking your home with Mrs. Meyers. My heart's been acting up on me again. Don was sent away to Pendleton Penitentiary, and Vilas went and joined the navy. I'll come to see you when I can. Why don't you ever write? Be a good boy.

Love, Mom

I crumpled the letter and flung it across the room. "I bet you'll come," I muttered. "Just like you promised to come get us when we were with Aunt Alice."

Not long after that I took things into my own hands, found a scrap of paper and stubby pencil in my room, and wrote,

34

Dear Welfare Lady,
    I want to be taken out of this home and moved. I can't stand to be with my foster brother and sister any more. If you don't move me, I'll run away.
                                    Sincerely,
                                    John Erwin

It frightened me that at eleven years of age I had made such a major decision. The welfare department, believing my threat, came to take me to another home. I had broken all family ties now, but I didn't care. I didn't want to see Louise again nor my mother nor anyone related to me. I had finally replaced the many hurts with a different emotion: hatred.

It was a bitter boy the social worker delivered that day to Amos Kelly's farm southwest of Greenfield, Indiana. I wondered immediately if I'd made a mistake. Old farm equipment in disrepair stood around the yard. I thought a good wind might destroy the sagging barn. A rusty, battered Chevy sat in the drive.

In spite of the poverty, however, I soon came to enjoy farming with Amos. We built a good comradeship, and their four-year-old son was no rival for me. The problem here was Amos's wife, Eleanor. She nagged and complained, and I hated her noisy chickens.

Often I'd hear Amos and Eleanor fighting.

"Eleanor, quit naggin' the boy s'much."

"Well, he won't even mind me. Jest sasses me all the time."

Amos would swear and Eleanor would scream. "Amos Kelly, I'll die before I ever take another welfare kid."

Secretly it pleased me to have them fighting over me, and I worked to find ways to increase her misery. On Sundays when they went off to visit friends, I quickly loaded a .22 and shot several of her chickens. Chuckling,

I loaded the corpses onto the tractor, drove far across the field, and dumped them where they'd never be found. I was sure I had committed the perfect crime.

When winter came and I spent more time around Eleanor, the friction between us increased, and we argued incessantly. Over and over, she threatened to call the social worker to come for me, which to a welfare kid was equivalent to calling the police.

In the barn one day, Amos turned to me, squinting in the smoke curling up from his cigarette, and said, "John, I like you."

Inside, I glowed to hear those words. I replied, "I like you, too, Amos."

"You're a hard worker, and you do real good work. You've been a big help t' me this year and a half. But you gotta calm down. You're 'bout to drive Eleanor crazy. She says she can't put up with you like you are."

"I really like it here, Amos, and I don't want to leave, but I jest can't change. I don't know why I can't get along with Eleanor."

"Well, if you can't change, you're gonna hafta leave."

"Then I guess I'll have to go."

I don't even know now where that next home was located. All I know is that those silent rides with the social worker between homes, cardboard suitcase on the seat beside me, were the longest hours of my short life. This time I landed with a crippled husband and his wife who earned their living caring for foster children, and I found a way to get the respect and attention I wanted. I became a bully. I pushed, I stole, I fought, I challenged the world to fight me back. The foster mother couldn't control any of us and was afraid to call the social worker. If the welfare department took us away, they'd lose their income. We knew it, of course, and made life unbearable for her.

At school, I would look around my seventh-grade class, hoping for a friendly glance, trying to discover if anyone might like me. I talked in the halls and on the playground, trying to be accepted, finding out who the bullies were. Carefully, I observed the invisible limits and boundaries made by classmates. But it was a painful, emotionally draining process, and I knew that any friends I made I would only leave in a few months.

When spring came, I passed a freshly plowed field with a tractor in the distance turning up black clumps of dirt, and I longed to be back farming with Amos. I wrote to him, begging him to take me back and promising to show Eleanor respect. Then each day I ran for the mail before anyone else, looking for a letter.

Finally, it came, the first letter I had received in two years. I ripped it open, holding my breath. Amos had decided to give me another chance.

That summer I prayed to God for help to make it this time, knowing I'd never get another chance. I knew I was walking on eggs. More than anything, I wanted to stay here, so I tried with everything in me. When Eleanor irritated me, I bit my lip so hard it hurt, sometimes until it bled. I resolved to make this home last.

The summer went fairly well, and I was happy with Amos, farming and enjoying the animals.

But after crops were gathered and colder weather forced us inside, the old problems resumed. I found it more and more difficult to bite my lip around Eleanor, to dam up the torrent of words I wanted to unleash. I felt I was losing my footing, sliding with nothing to hang onto.

One night when Amos was in Indianapolis selling a load of hogs, Eleanor sat with her visiting grandmother and me around the living room stove. I was cleaning and

37

oiling my hunting rifle, ramming the cleaning rod with the oiled cloth up and down inside the barrel, while the two women complained about me. Eleanor would make a caustic comment while grandmother rocked and nodded in agreement, now and then adding a few barbs of her own. Noticing that my retorts were becoming angrier, grandmother said, "Eleanor, we better shut up; he might decide to use that there gun on us."

The thought was planted in my mind, and after a while I couldn't restrain myself.

"Shut up, you -------! If you say another word to me, I'll kill you both!" They shut up, and I went to bed, over-joyed at my victory over those two nags. I had won.

Early the next morning my bedroom light was snapped on, my covers ripped off, and Amos struck me with his belt, yelling, "Git down to the barn!"

As the full impact of my threat against his wife and her grandmother dawned on me, I was petrified. Had I blown my chance? What would my punishment be? I dressed as slowly as I dared. Although Amos had never abused me, I had seen his temper on the rampage. When he called the cows in from the field and they wouldn't move, he would scream and curse and beat them with a pitchfork. Now, I wondered what punishment he might consider appropriate for a kid who had threatened to kill his wife.

In the barn I saw Amos pitching hay, and I closed my eyes and tightened my neck muscles.

"John," he called out sternly.

Then he leaned on the pitchfork and began to laugh uproariously.

"John, if I'd a-been you, I'd a-shot 'em both." My heart dropped back into my chest, and I blended my own laughter with his. Then we both roared until it was too painful to laugh anymore.

Then Amos's face changed abruptly, like a cloud covering the sun, and he said, "John, what makes you act like you do? Why can't you straighten up?"

He might as well have asked me how many grains of sand were on the seashore. I didn't know. What could I say? Why I resented Eleanor and why I could not get along with her, I had no idea. I had strained every fibre in my body to fit in here.

"I guess I just can't make it here, Amos. I'll have to leave."

Another failure. What good had it done to try? Or to pray? God hadn't helped me. During the next few days, waiting for the social worker, I played a popular Gene Autry song over and over. "Born to lose, I've lived my life in vain. . . ." I thought he must have written the song with me in mind.

Sandwiched between my smothering self-pity was my smoldering anger at myself. Why couldn't I adjust in my foster homes? I really wanted to, but I had no control. My emotions controlled me, and they were destroying me while I helplessly stood by.

I knew I was burning a bridge behind me, leaving the only home in thirteen years that I had liked and where someone liked me. Amos checked my room that day to make sure I hadn't forgotten anything, and I asked him if he knew where I was going.

"No, John, they didn't say."

THE END
OF THE
BANISTER

FOUR

I BELIEVE IN THE sovereignty of God. I know he's in his heaven, as the poet said; he's in control. And while I don't believe that he wills the pain and misery we suffer on earth, I know now at least that my own pushed-around childhood has contributed directly to my work as a chaplain. God has used it to a good end. I understand how deeply a man can be bent by his early bitter experiences.

Of course, the future benefit could hardly be seen as I went through the ordeal of a new school, filling out forms and being embarrassed by questions such as "What is your mother's maiden name? Age of your parents? Their places of birth?" I didn't know the answers and had no way to find out. In class it didn't take the students long to learn that I was a welfare kid. I felt as though I had a sign printed across my shirt—different, second class, a misfit.

I had left the farm this time for Indianapolis. There was one pleasant surprise, however. My brother Don, recently out of jail and divorced, began visiting me. I hadn't seen any of my family for years, and I basked in the thought that someone, especially someone in my family, actually wanted to be with me.

I had a Saturday job in a bakery now, and after work Don would take me to the large rooming house where he lived. I'd share dinner with him and the other boarders around a large table. No one asked questions. Here I was Don's brother. No one whispered, "Welfare kid," or passed sly looks to his neighbors. I belonged to someone, and it felt great.

Then I got the wild idea that perhaps I could live here. Surprisingly, the welfare department approved, appointing Don as my guardian and his landlady, who agreed to help supervise me, as co-guardian. I could scarcely believe that something I wanted had actually happened to me. I was thrilled to be near my own brother who cared about me. Finally I was getting a break in life.

Being with Don outweighed the disadvantage of having to start my third school this year. At first I tried to cooperate; I wanted to make good grades and act responsibly. I was even selected as a patrol boy. Perhaps if people looked at me as a good boy, I could change and start acting like one. But I soon began fighting anyone in my way, roaming the streets with a gang, skipping school, stealing bikes (the coveted status symbol during those World War II days), and coming back to Don at the rooming house with a smile and an air of innocence.

I tried to imitate Don in every way possible, copying his mannerisms and even his voice. When I skipped school, I'd return to Don's room to play records. When the telephone would ring, I would answer in Don's voice, "Hello."

"Mr. Erwin?"

"Yes."

"This is your brother's school calling. We are having some problems with John. He's not in school this afternoon and has been absent about eight days this month without an excuse."

"Well, thank you for telling me. I'll get on him and see that he goes to school as he should."

When report cards came out, I carefully applied ink eradicator to the number of days absent and changed it so Don wouldn't know. After he had seen the card, I changed the number back and returned it to school.

I was proud of Don, who worked for Canteen Company, servicing automatic vending machines. He wore a maroon jacketed uniform, an impressive outfit, and was known as the Canteen man. It must be grand to be recognized for something positive, I thought.

In the evenings, Don had another job, playing a trombone in a burlesque orchestra. He was a good musician, and he began to give me an occasional lesson on an old trombone he had. At school I started taking lessons, and though the trombone had no case, I carried it proudly. I was beginning to mend my shattered self-esteem. Someone cared for me, and I was learning that I could succeed in something. Perhaps life held something worth living for after all.

Then one evening the world I'd placed so much hope in blew up in my fourteen-year-old face. Don received a draft notice. I was far more stunned than he. I would lose him and have to move again, uprooted once more.

I managed to finish eighth grade while living temporarily with another half brother. Graduation was a highlight of my life; for once I was dressed like everyone else and looked like I really belonged. Although I despised my mother, I secretly hoped she would come. But she did not. None of my relatives were there to share my accomplishment.

Soon thereafter, I was sent to an orphanage, the Indianapolis Guardians' Home. My procession through seven foster homes had ended, and now at last I was in an institution—something I had always feared. Institutions meant control and loss of freedom—the end, it seemed, for I knew that kids almost never got out of institutions. No one wanted anyone our age with all our problems.

Often when I am counseling men in jail today, I can almost see the wheels turning in their heads. I know why they are trying to manipulate me and use me because I did the same thing. At the orphanage my bitterness drove me to lie and to sneer at authority to get what I wanted any way I could get it. For example, I had been smoking regularly for three years, so I asked for special permission to continue. I explained that I had just come in from the streets, was enslaved to the habit, and couldn't stop. My pleading was effective; I got permission to smoke outside, where I would not be seen by the others, who were not supposed to know about this arrangement.

Within weeks, of course, I had taught most of the others how to smoke. As one of the oldest kids there, I became a leader and taught them what I had learned while roaming the streets. I taught them that profanity meant prestige and politeness invited abuse. I showed them how to be a bully and how to fight.

I cringe now when I catalog the list of offenses I quickly piled up—shoplifting, vandalism, truancy, fighting. I roamed the city with a buddy or stole bicycles looking for trouble. If we weren't running through the giant Claypool Hotel smashing and destroying property in any unguarded room, we were at L. S. Ayres department store snatching money from the purses women had left for a few minutes in the record listening booths. Soon we could spot a house detective anyplace on the floor, and we'd race to the stairs with him in hot pursuit. The chase was a real thrill, and getting past the detectives at the exits was the challenge. Three times in three months I was expelled from Arsenal Technical High School, and an orphanage representative had to appear at school to reinstate me.

Late one afternoon after a day of disrupting the life of the citizens of Indianapolis, I heard the orphanage superintendent scream at me.

"John, there's someone to see you. Come down to the office." Her voice crackled up the stairs. She never just talked; she ordered, or screamed instead.

I hesitated at the top of the staircase. Not once during my six months here had someone come just to visit. People came to see me only when I was in trouble. Fear gripped me. This time I'd gone too far.

Clutching the wooden ball at the top of the rail, I thought I was going to be sick. I squeezed the ball and twisted it. It was loose in its socket, and the varnish had been worn off years before.

I stared at the familiar banister I had always wanted to slide down. Many times at school, when teachers were not around, I had happily zipped down banisters. But no one here would dare slide down this one.

My heart raced faster with each downward step. I had seen this coming. It was a collision toward which I had careened for years. But, oh, God, I wanted to avoid it. I hadn't intended to come to this. I wanted to cry, but mean, tough kids don't cry.

An urge to run seized me and seemed to push me toward the fire escape. But where would I go? No friends or relatives wanted me, and I knew I would just be caught again, sent back, and buried in more trouble. Slowly I trudged down the two flights, each step echoing through the ancient corridors. Now I must pull myself together

47

and not let these people know how I was hurting.

At the bottom of the stairs, I saw the somber-faced juvenile officer. I tried to act nonchalant and defiant.

"Put out your hands, boy," he said. I obeyed, while my eyes, filling with hatred, bored into his. He snapped on cold steel handcuffs, sending shivers all over my body. They were heavy enough to make my shoulders droop.

"Come on" was all he said.

We drove in silence to the juvenile detention home. As the car lurched to a stop, I looked at the rolled barbed wire atop the fences and the thick wire mesh on the windows. I was no longer just a troublesome orphan; I was a delinquent.

In the shower room, they forced me to strip, then squirted me with a foul-smelling disinfectant that burned all over. Next stop was a room where, from a huge barrel, I was handed a faded T-shirt with a YMCA logo on the front. Then I stepped into someone else's discarded, baggy pants and was sent to a dormitory.

My bravado was gone. Over the next two weeks I would lie in my bunk at night and pray, "God, please get me out. I'll be good, I'll straighten up—just please get me out of this place." I would cover my head with my pillow to muffle the crying.

Then the same juvenile detention officer returned to snap on the handcuffs again and lead me to court. The scene is still a nightmare for me. Judge Kay in his black robe sat high above us behind a desk that seemed the size of an ark. To my right I saw the assistant superintendent of the orphanage and the court reporter. The detention officer stood to the side as the judge told me to stand.

He then called on the orphanage representative to read the charges. The woman rose, wiped a few straggly gray hairs out of her eyes, and opened a little red book. She pursed her lips and began reading page after page of

48

accusations against me. Some I was guilty of and some I was not, but I was not allowed to say a word. Her high-pitched voice droned on and on; I thought she'd never stop. Finally she sat down and tucked the abominable little book into her purse.

The stern-faced judge waggled a long finger at me, and I trembled. He bellowed, "Young man, I don't see how any kid could be as mean as they say you are. But I am convinced that you will never make a satisfactory adjustment in life. You are hereby sentenced to White's Manual Labor Institute in Wabash, Indiana, for correction."

I stared at him in horror as he continued. "Why can't you be like all the good boys in Indianapolis? If you keep skipping school, you'll never get an education and can never live a productive life. You'll probably spend all your life in penal institutions."

WHITE'S

FIVE

I DON'T REMEMBER THE NAME of the juvenile officer who drove me to Wabash. We were together only two hours. But 32 years later I remember him, for he brightened one of the darkest days of my life. He seemed to trust me. He removed the handcuffs, and he didn't scold or berate me as the other juvenile officers had in past months.

I remember he stopped en route and bought me a Coke. Something about him earned my admiration and respect, and I hoped that someday I would be the kind of man he was. I think I can put my finger on it—he treated me like a regular person.

I heard a similar statement not long ago by an inmate at Cook County Jail. On Friday nights my wife and three children join me for a Bible study group at the jail. Our children have learned to love and accept the inmates, and they know it. The kids don't see skin color, nor do they categorize people in jail as criminals. They enjoy talking with inmate clerks; we often see them holding the hand of one or propping an arm on another one's shoulder or giving hugs or kisses good-bye. One night after class an inmate said, "Rev. Erwin, your kids are really somethin'. You'll never have any trouble out of them. Y' know, they treat us like . . . like we're regular people."

I know exactly what he meant. For a few fleeting moments I experienced warm, nonjudgmental acceptance from that officer. Then the gates of the institute closed him out of my life forever.

White's never had the infamous reputation of Cook County Jail, but I've often thought that few institutions could match its degrading, depraved, often sadistic treatment of a group of juveniles. And the irony was that it was owned and operated by an upstanding Protestant body.

I was assigned to two-story Curliss Cottage with thirty-five boys my age, given a bundle of used clothes with the number nine written in indelible ink inside each one, and told that here I was number nine. All my possessions would bear that number.

At exactly 5:30 the next morning, a shrill whistle jarred me awake. Seconds later, tall, burly Mr. Curliss came charging up the stairs swinging a narrow leather strap, his bushy gray hair flying. He looked like an avenging angel—or devil, I wasn't sure which. He ripped the covers off two boys still in bed and laid the strap on their bare legs.

We quickly made our beds, dressed, and scampered down to the basement bathrooms. Any loiterers received a smack with the strap. Before I knew it, Mr. Curliss was booming a warning, "You've got one minute left to finish washing up."

Next came the pre-meal time of silence and meditation—ten minutes. We hurried to a set of chairs, which were always kept in three neat rows. Of course, I had chair number nine, but I had no idea at this time how many miserable hours I would spend sitting on it. All the chairs were old and battered, and the backs were completely gone. Mr. Curliss sat at a desk in front, pencil in hand, his beady eyes darting back and forth along the rows of silent boys. Any sound, even a smile, would be punished at the end of the day.

Finally another whistle blew, and the somber Mr. Curliss led us to the front door. After he unlocked it, we walked single file to breakfast.

Here the regimentation was even more strict. The boys sat at one end of the dining room and the girls at the other, and neither were allowed to look toward the other while eating. Anyone caught disobeying this rule was slapped, and his number written down for later punishment.

Mealtimes were to be wordless. If we wanted food passed, we used hand signals. Four fingers meant bread; two fingers, crackers; stroking the thumb with the little finger, sugar or preserves; and crossed fingers, half glass of milk. Beyond that, we pointed to what we wanted. Leaving food on one's plate or milk in the cup was another punishable offense.

After I had been there a few weeks, tin cans replaced our drinking cups. A child accidentally broke a cup while washing dishes, and all of us were punished to "teach us responsibility." The cans had jagged rims, under which milk remained and curdled.

After breakfast that first day, I was assigned a job with the garden force under the supervision of my houseparent's son, just back from the army. Handed a short leather jacket worn thin and with one remaining button, I was told to go with my group across the snow-crusted field to the farm equipment shed. The temperature was near zero, and the wind blustered. At times I walked and at times I was blown across the field. Since I had no gloves, I shoved my hands in my pockets, but the wind would whip my jacket open.

That afternoon I entered White's unaccredited high school to study math, English, and typing. A student could attend four years there and never graduate with an acceptable diploma. When I realized this, I was furious at the judge who had sent me here, berating me for playing hooky and not getting an education. Now I could never get the education I needed. I have often wondered if that judge knew anything about this institution, and how many judges know the places to which they sentence people.

Evening punishment was the most agonizing time at White's. During my second day, I was caught talking during meditation, looking at a girl during class, and smiling while eating. The ever-watchful eyes saw, and number nine was written down three times. Throughout the evening meal, I and the others scheduled for punishment could hardly choke our food past the lumps in our throats. After forcing down the last bite, I marched reluctantly to the cottage and took my place on chair nine.

My mouth felt dry and my heart raced as a deep voice bellowed through the room, "Number nine—caught smiling during supper, two strokes; caught talking at meditation, three strokes; caught looking at a girl, four strokes."

I had seen the procedure the night before and knew what to do. I put my toes on the line painted on the floor, bent over, grabbed my ankles, and clenched my teeth.

Mr. Curliss had designed a paddle about two feet long, two inches wide, and a half inch thick, with four dime-sized holes drilled into one end. I don't know if he had it patented or not. He gripped the handle and held the paddle low so he could get a good upward swing. With what seemed to be all his brutish might, he struck my upturned buttocks, and I was literally lifted off the floor by the force. I swallowed a moan as the pain shot through my body. The next blows, I found, turned out to be not as painful, because the first one had had a numbing effect.

Back on chair number nine, I sat on my stinging backside and watched the other boys get theirs. No one snickered or smiled. That would bring more strokes. We simply boiled with anger as the paddle kept up its rhythm.

At the end came the masterpiece, so dreadful that today I hardly believe my memory. But I know it happened. They called it "corporal punishment for serious offenses." That day Neal had sassed the typing teacher, Miss Kemp. Mr. Curliss took him into a small linen room, then ordered him to strip completely naked and lie face down on a long wooden bench. One of the boys covered him with a wet sheet, because, as was piously explained, "Miss Kemp is a lady, and it would be a terrible sin for her pure eyes to behold the naked body of a boy."

When Miss Kemp came in, Mr. Curliss handed her a leather strap about two feet long and four inches wide. Silence hung in the air until we heard the ten snaps of the leather against the wet sheet and Neal's screams. Miss Kemp walked briskly past us and out of the room with the same detached expression she wore when she said, "Class, turn to page 38." I hated her.

Tom's turn was next. He'd been overheard saying, "Dammit," a ten-stroke offense. He, too, went into the corporal punishment room and stripped. I squeezed my ears, trying to block out the screams. Then Tom walked out, his shoulders twitching as he quietly sobbed. My eyes grew large as I noticed the red drops of blood spattering onto the floor. I stared with horror until Mr. Curliss bellowed:

"Nine! Get the mop and clean up!"

As I mopped, I watched Neal and Tom being forced to sign statements that they had been justly punished but that their skin had been neither bruised nor broken.

God's people did this, I told myself.

That night in bed I determined I would never get corporal punishment. Somehow I must manage to keep my body and mind from drifting apart. If I had to lick their boots, I would. I would say, "Yes, sir" and "No, sir" and pretend to agree and condone everything they said or did. I would convince them that they had reformed me. If I stroked them, they wouldn't stroke me. I would survive no matter how I had to lie and cheat to do it.

Sunday was the worst day of the week. After a boring, idle morning, we would have lunch and then march to church in two lines. Mr. Curliss would walk at the back, his hawklike eyes scrutinizing us all so he could record a number if anyone spoke, smiled, or broke a rule. We would sit quietly in the theater seats, appearing reverent while a minister from town made allusions to God's love. I didn't want to hear *any* talk about the love of God. I knew him only as a mean old man who liked to beat up kids who had no fathers. I wanted no part of him nor these cruel people, who were supposed to be his people. I'd rather have hell's angels on the outside any day.

Mr. Curliss sat at his desk with the mail while we sat on our familiar stools. He would pick up a letter and slowly censor it, reading it to himself, never telling us whom it was for. Instead, he'd read a few lines, then look up, read a few more lines and frown or look puzzled. Finally he would finish the letter, call out a name, and hand over the letter. Then he'd repeat this process with the next one.

Several months had passed, and I had never gotten a

letter. Then during one mail call, Mr. Curliss halted his usual provoking act and screamed, "Nine, get up here!" He scowled down at me and sneered, "What does your brother know about White's?"

"I—I don't know, sir. I haven't seen or written him since I've been here."

He jumped up, his huge bulk towering over me, and began slapping me around. His powerful hand boxed my ear, making my head ring. I jerked back, and he stepped close and buffeted me again and again.

"Y' know what your brother said?"

"No, sir," I answered, my head spinning.

"He said your ma is trying to get you in the Indiana Soldiers' and Sailors' Children's Home, which is probably better than the joint you're in. What does he mean calling this place a joint?"

I felt like saying I had better names than that for it. But I remembered my vow to myself. I would not let this man provoke me into saying something foolish.

About two months after Don's letter, I received the first visitor since I had lived here. The woman was a complete stranger, and she evaded my question when I asked why she had come to see me. Since we were in an office with several people, I asked her if we could go outside and talk. Sitting in her car, I pressed the question on my mind, "Are you from the Soldiers' and Sailors' Home?"

She hesitated and then said, "I was not supposed to tell you who I am. Yes, I am from the home. I am here to interview you about admittance."

I couldn't believe it. I was leaving White's!

But nothing happened. Several months went by, and I was tormented with the hope of leaving, a hope that never materialized. Then late one evening, I got the word to pack up. I put on what I had worn when I arrived, joyfully discarding all my number nine clothes.

As I left, the superintendent shook my hand. "I'm so sorry to see such a fine boy leave," he intoned. "You have done so well and really reformed." Tears ran down his cheeks. I was amazed. Couldn't he see the belligerence on my face or feel the deep hatred that poured out of me? I wanted to blurt out, "You cry, you fool, but you wouldn't let me cry. You wouldn't let me show any feeling of any kind the months I've been here. If I ever see you or anyone from this place on the outside, I'll make you pay for all the misery you caused me."

As an adult, many years later, I returned to White's Institute to show my family where I had once lived. As we drove onto the grounds, I was so overwhelmed with the pain of the past that I turned the car around and drove away as quickly as I could.

A CHOICE YOUNG MAN?

SIX

"WELCOME TO THE Indiana Soldiers' and Sailors' Children's Home. We hope you'll like it. Lemme take your bag."

The tone of voice sounded strange. For almost a year I had heard only harsh ultimatums. This cottage superintendent smiled as he spoke, and I couldn't remember the last time I'd seen a smile.

He looked a little like someone's grandfather, gray-haired and a little stooped. But I wasn't about to be taken in. I knew what people were like. That smile was a mask, and any minute, when I least expected it, he'd strike.

He led me upstairs and showed me my bed in a dormitory for about twenty-five. Then he said, "Why don't you go outside, John? Look around and meet some of the kids. When the whistle blows, come back here for lunch."

No lock on the door. No lines to march in. No threats. I stared at him for a moment, then quickly ran out onto the grass and down the hill before he changed his mind.

Down by the lake I met a group of children fishing and noticed the contrast. Rather than empty shells with glazed eyes, they were laughing, running, enjoying themselves.

It took me months to begin to relax and accept an environment of trust. I tried to bully the younger kids at first and got only disgust for a response. I started fights and stole gum, candy, pencils, anything left around. Rather than beatings, however, I got explanations of why I shouldn't behave that way and some mild punishment. When the social worker heard how I was acting, she warned me, "John, you're the first person from White's this home has ever admitted. You're treading on thin ice. If you don't turn things around, you could end up back in the reform school."

I tried to change. I honestly tried, but it seemed as though years of fighting the world from behind a wall of emotional armor was too much. All I could do was smash and destroy, but no one smashed back. As a result, the tight spring inside me began to relax little by little. It was here, during my high-school years, that my attitudes began to change and the sun began to shine once again.

Mr. and Mrs. Todd, who were in charge of recreation, were the kind of people who were almost always available to talk, to laugh, to have fun with us. On Friday nights they supervised a free time of roller skating, basketball, and dancing; Mrs. Todd ran the canteen. Stuffed chairs lined the walls of one large room, and we spent hours there just talking and listening to the juke box.

These were the days when FM radio was just coming along, and since I was studying electronics in school, Mr. Todd paid me the ultimate compliment: he asked me to build an FM antenna. My self-esteem took a dramatic climb, especially when I got the thing finished and it worked.

64

The band conductor gave me a brand-new Conn trombone, and I found I could often work out my feelings through music. In a few months I won first chair, and stayed there throughout my four years. Later, I won the job of drum major, and I saw I could get attention by excelling.

I would have chosen Mr. and Mrs. Todd for parents if I had had any say in it. They balanced firmness and discipline with love and concern, all of which I needed in generous measure. They taught me to use my head instead of my fists.

As my high-school graduation neared, I felt the mixed emotions of leaving the first place I ever wanted to call home and making it on my own in the big world. I would no longer be a ward of the court, and the home had no choice but to send me out. Since I had worked the last two summers for an electrician, the Hancock County Rural Electric Cooperative in Greenfield, Indiana, promised me a job at graduation. That brought me one step closer to a secret dream I had lived many times in my mind. Some day I would be a power lineman.

The world knows Greenfield as the birthplace of the poet James Whitcomb Riley. I remember it as the friendly little industrial town where I entered the working world on my own. My brother Don helped me to find a room in a boarding house, where a motherly woman watched over my social life, my grooming, and my personal habits. I had got this far in life without the help of a mother, and I didn't feel I needed one now, so after a few months I found another room on my own.

I began work at the power company as a grunt, the guy who does the dirty work for the more experienced linemen, and I thought my 135-pound body would collapse in the process. During my first months we built new power lines in rural areas, and although we had power equipment to dig holes for the poles, the dirt had to be tamped by hand. Sometimes I thought my arms would fall off if I tried to lift that tamp one more time. But I loved the work, and my body finally agreed to join my brain and work harmoniously. Eventually, I hoped to move to the power distribution centers, where I could work on high-tension lines on steel towers all across the country.

My fellow workers were good to me and taught me the trade. I learned to take pride in my work, to be punctual, and I became an accepted member of the team. They didn't look upon me as different or inferior, and, for the first time, I felt a part of something good in regular society.

The feeling of independence also buoyed me. I had my own room, rather than being in a dorm with twenty-five others. I bought my own soap, toothpaste, towels, and clothes rather than having them furnished by the taxpayers. I wanted to shout to the world, "Look, you taxpayers, I'm paying taxes now, and I'm buying my own things. I'm on my own."

My ego still needed support, however. I was embarrassed that the landlady could see how little mail I was getting. So I rented a post office box. Later I got the idea to fill in all the advertising forms I could find for free literature, and when the box filled with third-class mail, I made sure my landlady noticed. At least someone knew John Erwin was alive.

(Recently a former inmate told me a similar story. Lonely and apart from the world, he wrote letters to himself while in prison. When the guards brought his mail, he pretended that someone out there cared enough about him to write.)

Although the emptiness in my life still gaped, I became comfortable in Greenfield, making surface friendships, enjoying my work. I was finding some happiness here and doing it all by myself, and it was a good feeling. It lasted more than a year and a half. Then one day, I found a first-class letter in my box. Excitedly I ripped it open to read, "You are one of America's choice young men." Someone needed me . . . to help resolve the Korean conflict. I was drafted.

Angrily I squeezed the letter into a ball and threw it. Why me? Why ruin my life now that I was finally paying my own way? Let the army take the rich kids, the ones who'd lived in good homes all their lives. I wanted to cry, but my tear ducts had run dry long ago. Instead, bitterness and anger oozed from me.

I sold my prized TV and phonograph, stored my trombone and record collection, threw away my clothes and other possessions, and said good-bye to the men I worked with. On a cold, gray February day, half-drunk and in total despair, I packed a few belongings and cursed the day I was born.

My landlady tried to console me, saying, "Now, John, this is no way to feel and act."

"Mind your own business," I bellowed. "It's my life and I'll live it like I please." Swearing, I stumbled down the stairs on my way to induction at Fort Custer, Michigan. If only I'd known that one day I would return to Greenfield a radically different young man looking forward to life in that small town.

"WE'RE GONNA TEACH YOU HOW TO KILL"

SEVEN

I'VE SEEN AND TALKED to more lonely men in my lifetime than most people, and I know that the need for friendship and concern and approval will drive a man to uncharacteristic behavior. As a chaplain, if I counsel twenty hardened convicts a day, I know I could get twenty conversions with the right tactics. After preaching to a cellblock of sullen, resentful prisoners, I could have almost every man there on his knees asking for forgiveness. Loneliness coupled with the chain of guilt most of these men drag around leads them to think about God and often try religion in some form.

As a young soldier, I had that same aching loneliness and oppressive guilt, covered with a layer of fear of being sent to war. I had heard of thousands of U.S. soldiers killed in Korea, and I wondered if even God would know if my life ended on a cold Korean battlefield.

The impersonal processing of new soldiers didn't help my depression. I received a number and a uniform. When other recruits wrapped up their civilian clothes and sent them home, I stuffed mine in a trash can. Who

71

would I send them to? Because of my work with the power company, I was assigned to the signal corps, sent to Camp Gordon near Augusta, Georgia, and enrolled in courses in electricity.

There, on a hot, dry parade ground, an old bulldog sergeant bellowed at us, "We're gonna teach you how to kill." Now I was not only lonely, I was afraid.

We were soon given twelve complex general orders to memorize. I'd never been able to memorize lists of facts, and try as I might, I could never get through the twelve. I seemed to have a giant mental block. During one inspection, as we stood at attention like tin soldiers, the commanding officer marched up and down the lines, choosing a different order for each soldier to recite. When he got to me, he squinted at me and roared, "Soldier, what's your fifth general order?"

Staring into space like a wooden Indian, I searched my brain for the answer that wasn't there. Finally, I blurted out, "I don't know, sir."

"Put that man on KP," he growled to the sergeant behind him.

The scene repeated itself four or five times for the next few weeks until, to my great relief, we were given another assignment to memorize, the chain of command. Tired of peeling potatoes and washing dishes, I sat up nights going over and over the chain of command until I knew it backwards and forwards. Secretly I looked forward to the next inspection so I could shock the commanding officer.

When the inspection came, I stood proudly in line, a confident smirk on my face. I could hear the officer's voice blaring at each soldier as he came down the line, citing a section of the chain of command for them to recite. At last he stood before me, squinted as before, and roared:

"Soldier, what's your fifth general order?"

That night as I put the peeler the thousandth time to a dirty potato, I wondered about the sadistic clairvoyance of that officer.

Every soldier received a small New Testament from the Gideons, and I looked on mine with some confusion. I'd always thought King James wrote the Bible. But this one said Gideon on the cover. So Gideon and King James must have collaborated on writing it. That's how little I knew.

But I began to read it anyway. Flipping through the pages, I soon came to the Book of Revelation and began to plow through the dark catastrophic judgments and horrors. It shocked me I had had a tough life on earth, but I had seen nothing yet compared to this. God was storing up these horrible punishments to unleash on me after I was shot and killed in Korea.

One Sunday in the post chapel I heard a scholarly minister in a black robe preach a sermon in which he explained that the Book of Revelation was written in figurative language. That was some relief, but I couldn't completely shake the thought that perhaps he was wrong. My obsession with death remained, and I looked for religion in any form I could find it. I had heard about men at war who had carried a New Testament in their shirt pocket and stopped a bullet that way. So I religiously carried mine in my left shirt pocket, little realizing that my heart was actually several inches to the right. I would have died of fright if I'd known that. I also bought an expensive sterling silver cross to wear on a chain around my neck. Between the New Testament and the cross, surely I'd be safe in Korea.

But Bible reading, chapel attendance, and prayer seemed to have little effect in getting God's attention. It was all one way; I heard nothing from heaven. When I got my first leave from the post after eight weeks of basic training, I decided to try a civilian brand of religion. Perhaps the Christians of Augusta, with their splendid church buildings and stained-glass windows, had something going with the Almighty. I knew nothing about denominations and doctrine, so I chose a church of the group to which my mother belonged. I never thought she was right about anything else, but at least I'd give her religion a try.

Surely God must be in this place, I thought as I sat in that padded pew and listened to the magnificent tones of the organ. After the service, Southern hospitality took over, and I soon became a part of this upright and proper group of God's people.

Just the same, I wasn't getting anywhere. My nagging fear of death plus the bags of guilt I carried with me everywhere still depressed me. I was determined to approach the youth leader, a pleasant young man who seemed to have answers for everything, and plotted for three weeks to meet him in the hall after the youth meeting. My plan worked, and as I stopped him, I summoned my courage and politely asked him, "May I talk to you?"

"Certainly." He smiled at me.

The words stumbled out as I explained to him how lonely and afraid and empty I was and how I desperately wanted peace with God.

He looked at me for a moment, cleared his throat, and then intoned, "John, you're at a crossroads in life, and whatever you do, I hope you take the right road. Please excuse me now. I must attend to the evening service." And he went off down the hall.

I stood gaping after him, angry at him, at God, at myself, at my mother. Stamping away, I cursed God and slammed the door to his house, vowing I'd never set foot inside another church the rest of my life.

While I gave up the search for God outwardly, my days of fear, depression, and loneliness were almost over. Meanwhile, the time dragged as we drilled, trained, and prepared for war off in that obscure peninsula in the Far East. Our company commander had told us, "I'm a second lieutenant. I'm gonna make first lieutenant, and you men are gonna make it for me." So we spent long hours shining everything that didn't move, whitewashing the rocks and the curbs, and sweeping the sandy grounds around the buildings. We knew that if we could use this company commander for bayonet practice, we'd learn to kill a lot faster.

JOHN THE BAPTIST

EIGHT

YOU WAIT A LOT in the army. You stand in line for food, for inspection, for pay. You stand in line just so they can count to see if everyone is in line. If you're not standing at attention, you're shuffling from one foot to another, mind in neutral. You're in no hurry. When you get to the end of this line, there's something else to wait for.

While in one of these lines, I devised a plan to thwart what I suspected was God's plan to have me killed in Korea. If I could do well enough on my courses in electronics, I could stay on at Camp Gordon as an instructor. Wits, that was it. You had to use your wits. When the final test came, I wrote every note I could on my fingernails with a sharp pencil, rubbed it off as soon as I'd used the information, then waited.

Finally, orders were posted. My plan had worked. While most of the company had instructions to report for shipping to the Far East, I simply moved my gear to a new barracks down the road as one of the privileged instructors.

The preoccupation with death faded a little after that, but an empty spot remained. Searching around to fill it, I turned to music, sent for my trombone, and joined the post dance band. With that familiar instrument in my hand, tonguing and sliding my part of a Stan Kenton or Tommy Dorsey arrangement, I was as close to happiness as I had ever been in my life.

I still hated the army, especially the inspections. This camp and our company in particular was a showplace for the army, and I got KP one time for not having the bottom of my boots shined. So, naturally, another plan I often devised was a way to get out of inspection, and that meant a trip to the dispensary for some imaginary illness.

It was on one of those Saturday mornings that I picked up a copy of the *Camp Gordon News* blowing across the parade ground. I had time to kill, not wanting to arrive back at the barracks while the officers were checking brass buttons and measuring sideburns, so I sat on a nearby bench to read. A front-page article about Augusta's civic symphony orchestra caught my attention. They needed trombonists. A few days later I went for an audition.

I'm not a mystic, so even today I find it hard to explain what happened that evening. I have to believe that while I had given up on God, he hadn't given up on me, and the events of the next few minutes were part of a plan that would eventually change my life. I noticed a small man with wiry black hair sitting in the trombone section. There was nothing unusual about him, but immediately I said to myself, *That man has the answer to life, and I'm going to get it somehow.* I walked over and held out my hand.

"I'm John Erwin."

"Dave Pitman," he responded. Unemotional, he

THE MAN WHO WHO KEEPS GOING TO JAIL

John with his sisters (Joan, center; Louise, right) and the dog Jack at foster home number one—Aunt Alice and Uncle Frank's.

John's daily chores included milking a rather strange cow.

At the age of eight, he could still smile, at least for the camera.

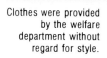

Clothes were provided by the welfare department without regard for style.

As a fearful GI during the Korean War years, John spent off-duty hours in the Augusta (Ga.) civic orchestra. It was there that he (back row, far left) met the man who helped change his life—Dave Pitman (back row, far right).

Dell Erwin

The Scripture on Erwin's office wall calls Christians to show a special concern for prisoners. He has been doing that now for 25 years.

When Erwin realized his men needed more than preaching, he launched PACE Institute, a blend of job training, remedial education, and counseling.

An inmate listens during a group Bible study.

One-to-one counseling in the cellblocks.

The Erwin children join their parents at the inmates' Friday night dialogue group.

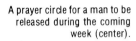

A prayer circle for a man to be
released during the coming
week (center).

Automotive (above)
and electronics repair
(above right) are but
two of the job skills
taught by PACE staff
and volunteers to help
inmates get ready for
life on the outside.

hardly smiled. Yet I couldn't shake the idea that an aura of peace surrounded the man.

I listened to him during rehearsal. He played difficult passages with skill and precision, and I admired him.

Several weeks later at rehearsal I commented to him, "I wish I could play the way you do."

"Would you like a few lessons, John? Come over to the house. No obligation, of course. Be glad to teach you what I know."

Why should he waste his time on someone like me? I didn't know, but before he could change his mind or back out of it, I answered, "I sure would."

That's how I found myself in Dave Pitman's home, sharing meals with his wife, Rozzie, and their two children, soaking up the family life and the unexplainable peace that surrounded them both. They never talked about it. They didn't act superior, like they knew something or had something I didn't. It was just there, and whatever it was, I wanted it.

Going to Korea seemed such a remote possibility these days that I hadn't thought much about death until I received a telegram. My half brother Ed, just forty-two, had died of a heart attack. There had been no warning; he hadn't even been ill. The old fear and the thoughts of judgment rushed to mind, and I realized I had only buried them unsuccessfully.

Ed was really a stranger to me, but I clung to some unexplainable need for a family, so I applied for a leave and made the long train ride to Indianapolis for the funeral. I could usually contain my emotions—I'd learned to hide them all too often to save my skin—but at my brother Don's house I let go and wept uncontrollably.

"I can't go back," I cried. "I can't go back. I hate it, and I'm miserable."

"You have no choice, John." Don put his hand on my

shoulder, helped me to pull myself together, and took me to the train. I thought the long ride back was the worst I could bear, but only months after that I got another telegram. This time it was Earl, another half brother, also in his forties, dead from a heart attack.

I sat on my bunk, and waves of hot then cold swept over me. I perspired, and I could feel my own heart, like I held it in my hand, beating steadily, waiting for some unknown signal to stop and take me to the same grave with Ed and Earl.

I couldn't face another funeral. I kept seeing my own face staring up at me from a casket—cold, white—and a company of strangers silently filing by. This time before I left, I called Dave Pitman. "I have to talk to you, Dave. When I get back, I have to ask you some questions." If he did have something or knew something that other people didn't know, I was going to find out. Only the thin thread of hope that Dave and Rozzie had some answers sustained me through the trip to Indiana.

Back at the base I put away the last shirt from my overnight bag and raced to the phone in the company day room.

"Dave, this is John. I need to talk to you."

"Fine—why don't you meet us at our church on Sunday? Then you can come back to our house and spend the day."

I agreed and slowly eased the phone to its cradle, greatly disappointed. *Don't tell me all he has to offer is church!* I thought. I had planned never to go to church again, and if anybody but Dave Pitman had invited me, I would have quickly told him where he and his church could go. But Dave had spent nearly a year demonstrating that he genuinely cared about a nobody like me. I admired him, and I would have met him anywhere or anytime.

82

So I overcame my contempt for church and met him and his family the next Sunday. He introduced me to most of the people there, and they seemed to know me. I couldn't figure it out, but most puzzling of all was that these people seemed to have the same quality of life Dave and Rozzie had. My hope began to build.

The next weekend I sat in the big stuffed chair in the Pitmans' living room. Guardedly and with fumbling words, I tried to tell Dave and Rozzie how I felt inside. They knew nothing of my scarred past. I had carefully concealed it, knowing that if they were aware of what a terrible person I was, they would never have me in their home or around their children. If they knew all the garbage I hauled around inside, they'd surely feel degraded in my presence. I tried to explain to them the great loneliness I had had for as long as I could remember and how mixed-up I felt. I told them how I had tried to contact God but never seemed to get near him, and about the guilt I carried with me.

They both got Bibles and knelt beside me, one on each side, showing me verses such as Romans 3:23, which says everyone has sinned. They explained that sin is missing God's goal for our lives, that it separates us from him. Christ died for my sins, they said. Then they turned to John 3:16 and read that God loved the world, including me, and that by trusting his Son, Jesus, I could have a new kind of life. They explained that Christ loved me personally, had died for me, and could change my life.

Dave and Rozzie had never talked directly to me about God or the Bible during the months I had known them. I probably would have run from them if they had. I wasn't ready then, but now I was.

I had heard all these things many times before. I had listened to many sermons about God loving me and Christ dying for the sins of humanity, but I could never make it mean much to me. But now, here was a man and woman who had loved me for almost a year. They had loved me without a cause, and if God were anything like the Pitmans, he must be able to love me without a reason, too.

Down on my knees beside them I prayed, asking Christ to forgive my sins and take control of my life. When I stood up, I saw tears streaming down Rozzie's cheeks. She hugged me while Dave just stood there beaming. But I didn't feel anything. I didn't seem any different. I didn't see flashing lights, didn't hear angels singing or bells ringing, but I believed Christ had accepted me, and I had accepted him. I'd just have to trust him for the rest, hang on, and see what would happen.

"Your sins are forgiven, John," Dave kept saying. "You don't have to carry that guilt anymore. Trust God now."

"Dave, it sounds too good to be true." But he said it was, and more importantly, the Bible said it. "I'm going to believe it," I finally concluded.

The emotional upheaval I looked for never happened, but that was all right. For most of my twenty-two years I had tried to live on emotions and feeling, highs and lows, and had found them as unreliable as a broken compass. They had carried me high and dropped me hard.

Now I would trust what the Bible said, because Dave and Rozzie said it was true. All I understood about God at this point was in the lives of these two people. I didn't need to understand how he created the world or how he became a man. I didn't need to understand all the doctrines of the Bible. Right now, it was enough for me to believe that my sins were forgiven and my guilt could go.

The next morning I awoke filled with the consciousness of the decision made the day before. I walked to the window. The sky was no bluer; the grass no greener; I still felt no different. I was still in the army, which I hated with vehemence. Yet I held onto the fact that, according to the Bible, I was a free person for the first time in my life. I *was* different, and I kept reminding myself of that.

Dave and Rozzie had given me some books, and between classes and inspections and waiting in lines, I found time to read them. I pulled out my New Testament from the foot locker where I had stuffed it long ago and began to underline passages Dave and Rozzie suggested. Slowly I realized something was changing. Old doubts were fading. I was looking at life differently. I had a reason to live. The hole inside was filled. I talked to God and knew that he heard me. I began to learn more about him.

To get to the Pitmans' church in Augusta meant walking a mile to the bus stop on the post, changing to another bus in town, and then walking another mile. However, I attended every church meeting they held—prayer meetings, youth meetings, worship and preaching services. I carried my Bible with me, not as a good-luck charm to ward off evil this time, but because in it I was finding answers to my needs.

At the base my friends were convinced there was a girl in church I was trying to impress. I spent the weekends with Dave and Rozzie and moved my civilian clothes and most possessions there. It became my home, and they were like a family to me. I even found that I became a better, more conscientious instructor, and I spent extra time giving individualized instruction.

Someone in the barracks long ago had tagged me "Little John." Now they gave me a new name, "John the Baptist." Oddly enough, I didn't mind it. I couldn't have handled any kind of rejection before, but now I was accepted by God and learning to accept myself. It was his approval that really mattered.

I learned, however, that not everything the guys said

should be brushed off. One night after prayer meeting, I went to the late-night meeting place, the latrine (the only lighted area), where soldiers met just to talk. When the talk drifted to religion, one soldier turned to me and said, "Hey, John the Baptist, what kind of Christian are you anyway, skipping parades and inspections?" I didn't have an answer. My conscience knew he was right, and after that, I never missed another parade or inspection, no matter how much I detested them.

At Bethany Chapel I found the same love and acceptance Dave and Rozzie offered. These people cared about me. Being with them, I felt a depth of affirmation I had never experienced before. Like a giant sponge, I soaked up all this love and knowledge about God.

In this church, laymen were given many opportunities to take part, and I began to pray in public and share thoughts at the weekly Communion service. People encouraged me by saying things like "John, your prayer was a blessing to me." "I appreciated what you had to say during the service, John." "It's great to have you with us."

But over and over I heard a comment that stuck in my mind. "John, I believe the Lord has something special for you to do. God is going to use you in some unique way, I know."

They could afford to be optimistic—they didn't know about my past. I had locked the door on that part of me. I couldn't share those hurts and shame with anyone, and although I felt complete acceptance from these people, I was not sure how they'd react if they knew about my former life. Fifteen years later, Dave and Rozzie attended a banquet where I had been asked to share my life's story. For the first time they heard about my foster homes and childhood experiences. Throughout my talk Rozzie wept uncontrollably and found it incredible that the John I was telling about was the one they knew.

When summer came, I attended a Bible conference in the Blue Ridge Mountains, learning more about God and the Bible and enjoying the fellowship of other believers. Basking in these beautiful surroundings and feeling a bond with all these people was like being in heaven, and I never wanted to leave. God continued healing me, and I became more firmly entrenched in my desire to serve him and make my life a blessing to others.

Eventually, only one month remained in my two-year army stint. After training my successor, I had a lot of spare time these final days, so I spent it in the repair shop fixing equipment. One by one the soldiers I worked with, many of whom had laughed at me, came in to talk, telling how much they respected me for my changed life. Even a man named Fryberg, who had a reputation as the toughest guy in the company, came in. He had harassed me incessantly. We talked for a long time, and as I told him my story, the tears came to the eyes of this tough guy. "I wish I could believe," he told me. "But I just can't."

I couldn't find the job I wanted in Augusta, so I decided to return to my old one in Indiana. Late one cold, blustery February afternoon, I stopped to say good-bye to Dave and Rozzie. They had loved me without a cause, befriended me, fed me, counseled me, given me free trombone lessons, and led me to a decision that had given my life meaning. I could never thank them enough.

I finally pulled myself away and, with trombone case and duffle bag, headed for my car. I had gone only a few steps and turned back for something I'd forgotten. At the top of the steps was Rozzie—I still can see the image today—with tears streaming down her beautiful face.

On my way north, I stopped in Kentucky for what I hoped would be a strategic visit: to see my mother. Her house was covered by a tin roof that had lost its gloss many years ago. The wooden steps creaked beneath me as I knocked on the door. We exchanged the customary Southern greeting—a quick hug, more like a salutation than an expression of love.

The conversation was friendly enough, but inside I was confused. It was hard to feel that this woman was my mother. I was thankful to be free of my hatred for her, but we never broke free to share with each other how we really felt about the past.

I'd written her a number of letters in recent months about my new faith, but when I brought up the subject now, she only rocked faster in her rocker and said, "Now, John, you're new at this religion business. I've been a Christian for many years, and I know a lot more about it than you do. So don't be tryin' to set me straight."

I would see her only once more, shortly before her death in 1955.

Greenfield looked the same after two years. It was still little more than a place to slow down the truckers on their Indianapolis-to-Dayton runs. But I had changed, and now the people seemed different to me. I had left as a lonely, frightened young man. I returned with confidence in myself and a genuine deep joy of life. I had written to my friends at the Hancock County Rural Electric Membership Corporation to tell them about my new faith, and the secretary greeted me with, "Well, John Erwin, of all the people in the world to be converted, I never expected you!"

I could smile now at a comment like that. I had experienced God's love, and I could care for others now. Greenfield was no longer a hostile spot on the map in which I had to chip out a place to live. The people at the electric corporation and my landlady and the truckers on Route 40 were just needy people like myself.

One of my jobs was to read electric meters in rural areas, which meant I spent hours driving around the country. I studied my Bible during lunch and any leisure time I could find.

That wasn't enough, however. I somehow wanted to make up for the twenty-two years of my life that I'd lived without knowing God, so I packed my few belongings and moved once again. Dave and Rozzie had recommended a place to study in Oak Park, a suburb of Chicago, so in September, 1954, I landed on the doorstep of Emmaus Bible School.

Many of the Emmaus students had grown up in Sunday school and knew the names, places, and stories of the Bible backwards and forwards. I had a little trouble placing which Joseph and which Saul in which Testament, but I was determined to learn. Like a blotter I soaked up everything I could. I had trouble memorizing the names of the kings of Judah and Israel or the dates of the church councils, but the Book began to take on meaning for me. I grasped the precepts, the lessons, the meaning of the stories and events, and I clung to the prophecy of the Christians back in Augusta that God had something special for me someday. I sincerely wanted to find God's will for me, and I never doubted that I'd find it.

LIGHT FOR A DARK PLACE

NINE

BACK IN THE 1950s, a man named Wesley Kosin cared deeply for the men inside Cook County Jail. A gray-haired distinguished-looking Protestant chaplain, he quietly counseled scores of prisoners each month, conducted worship services on Sunday morning, and faithfully spread the Word of God through the tiers.

Kosin was not a crusader, however. The prison rules under which he worked were strict, but Kosin didn't push them. Warden Jack Johnson liked Kosin. The chaplain wore baggy clothes and scuffed shoes he had bought secondhand, and he was a humorless, conservative man. But he was also gifted and intelligent, and he worked with a conviction that God had called him to bring the gospel to the unfortunate men behind bars.

Kosin came to Emmaus Bible School one spring day in 1955 to tell the students about prison work and enlist their support. This challenged me immediately, and I signed up to help him with the Sunday morning services on the cellblocks.

I had been in jails before. The August before, I had gone with the church people to visit prisoners. I had heard of Cook County Jail but could never imagine it.

It was awesome, even from the outside, with its massive stone wall and watchtowers and imposing steel doors. The guards searched everyone going in, even the Christians with their Bibles and smiles and hopeful hearts. Then the door slammed behind us, and down the corridor I could see hands, scores of hands, hanging onto the bars. As I walked, the faces appeared, each one looking out at us from behind the bars.

I thought back to the day nine years before when I was taken in handcuffs and locked in the juvenile detention center. I remembered now what it felt like. I understood the despair behind the blank faces that stared at us, the loneliness, and the guilt. I had a panicky overwhelming feeling of a loss of freedom, but the knowledge that I could help these men buoyed me. I wanted to shout down the long steel hall, "You can be free! Listen—Jesus Christ can set you free." Instead, I followed Chaplain Kosin and the guard with our group of seven into an archaic, creaky elevator that rumbled up two flights and deposited us in a control room outside a cellblock.

I've gone through this ritual countless times now, and it's always the same. Sixty or so men sit around a dayroom about forty feet square. A few men playing cards or dozing in a corner ignore you. Most of them look to you expectantly. If you watch carefully, you can see who runs the cellblock. He'll stand up first to pull a bench around, and all the others will follow. If, however, he ignores you, only a small group will form, hesitantly, driven by some deep longing to risk the wrath of the leader. Some church groups have even had water thrown on them.

I remember one time a burly black man rose and announced to us, "I'm Hatchet Face." Then he told his cellmates, "We're gonna have church. Pull these benches around." They obediently clustered into a semicircle facing us, like disciples at the feet of a master.

Those were the times I was thrilled to stand up and preach. I had slowly, hesitantly gained the confidence to stand before a group. My grammar had always been poor, and I could never come up with those seven-point alliterative sermon outlines my fellow students took pride in, but in the jail it didn't matter. I knew the language. I felt I understood the men, and they understood me. I began working at Cook County Jail on Saturdays as well, counseling men under the expert guidance of Chaplain Kosin.

Not all my free time, however, was spent in the jail. That same March I got up enough courage to date one of the popular girls at Emmaus. Dell was a long-haired Alabama girl with just the right amount of soft Southern accent and all the right answers in class. I waited until I had saved enough to buy a '52 Pontiac, sure that she wouldn't consider dating anyone without a car.

After our first ride around Oak Park on a Friday afternoon, I waited several weeks before asking her out again. This time it was a Sunday afternoon drive, during which we studied for a test in Biblical Introduction. She practically had the textbook memorized, and I was thoroughly impressed. She was intelligent, attractive, and fun to be with, and we dated steadily. Still, I kept my guarded approach.

At the end of school, I was invited to go to Michigan to assist the electrician I had worked with during the school year. Unsure whether to go or to stay and work with Chaplain Kosin, I prayed and decided Michigan was where I belonged. Dell and I corresponded regularly, and my feelings towards her were deepening. In her letters I looked for a hint of her feelings but found none.

She gave me no reason to think I was anything more than a friend.

After several weeks, I felt uncomfortable in Michigan. Was this really how I was supposed to be spending my summer? An internal conflict built until I thought I could stand it no longer. One night I climbed to my room in the third-floor attic of the farmhouse where we were staying and told God just how I felt. I knew I could be honest without fear of provoking him. "God, I just don't understand this. I'm as miserable as can be, and I'm going to stay in this room until I get an answer from you."

As I read the Bible that night, I stopped at Genesis 32:9 and read, "Return unto thy country, and to thy kindred, and I will deal well with thee." It seemed that God was speaking to me through this passage, not in an audible voice, but through my mind.

I couldn't understand what it meant, however. My country? My kindred? I had lived in seventeen different places by now, so where would I return? The only application that seemed feasible was that I should go back to Emmaus and work in the jail.

But Mr. Brooks, my employer, had a harsh temper, which I'd seen many times during the months I had worked with him. He'd be furious with me for leaving in the middle of the summer, and I shuddered to think of the explosion I would trigger. I became more and more convinced that I should leave, however, so I prayed, "Lord, if you will hold Mr. Brooks's tongue when I tell him I'm leaving, then I'll know for sure it's your will."

The next morning I opened my dry mouth to tell him but quickly closed it again in fear. Several attempts later I blurted, "Mr. Brooks, I believe God would have me return to Emmaus and work in the jail." I held my breath, not daring to look at him, waiting for the tirade to begin. I wanted to hide under the table.

Casually, he answered me. "Well, John, if you feel that's God's will, then that's what you should do. Tomorrow I'll help you get ready to go."

Slowly I exhaled and thanked him, but he did not know how thankful I was.

Back at Emmaus, I contacted Chaplain Kosin, who told me, "My wife and I have been praying for someone to take my place at the jail this summer so we can study linguistics with Wycliffe Bible Translators." So there *was* some explanation to why God wanted me back in Chicago!

The rest of that summer I counseled three days a week and conducted Sunday services, plus an evening Bible class. In order to make ends meet, I worked the other three days as an electrician out of IBEW Local 134. Jail chaplains, unlike prison chaplains, are not paid by the government; they serve strictly on a missionary basis. Chaplain Kosin (and later I myself) belonged to the Light Bearers Association of America, an organization for ministry in institutions. But we still had to come up with our own funds.

We had no office to talk to men back then. We interviewed inmates on the cellblocks, with a heavy steel partition and a twelve-inch square glass window separating us. We both had to yell for any type of communication. On top of that, we had to override the noises of sixty other inmates in the background.

Meanwhile, Dell and I continued to date, and I thought I was falling in love. But I had been in love so many times. How could I be sure? She had a substance and character I had not found in other girls. She wasn't fickle; she had a commitment to do the Lord's will and showed a willingness to sacrifice, to give up material possessions and money if necessary. Wanting to be sure of the Lord's leading, I prayed much and waited.

97

In the fall, Chaplain Kosin returned to Cook County, and I went back to school full time, still assisting at the jail. By November I was sure Dell was God's choice for my wife, and one evening in the student lounge, I took the plunge. The strict social rules of a Bible school in the 1950s being what they were, I held her hand under a newspaper (so none of the staff could see we were touching). Inhaling deeply, I said, "Dell, I love you enough to marry you."

"I love you, too."

"Well, what's your answer?"

"You didn't ask me a question."

"Could you . . . I mean . . . will you be my wife?"

We couldn't kiss or hug in this public place surrounded by other students and an ever-watchful staff who forbade any public display of affection. A tight hand squeeze, carefully hidden, sealed our commitment to one another.

It happens every day, I know. Couples get engaged and know the intoxication of being in love. But there was something else for me. For the first time that I could remember, I would belong exclusively to some other person, and someone would belong to me.

On June 1, 1956, after the spring semester had ended, we were married at her home in Alabama. We honeymooned for a week in Mobile. Then I took Chaplain Kosin's place again for the summer, working three days a week and going to the jail three days. Dell took a job to become the major breadwinner for the family. The thought of getting rich never entered our heads. We were content to have each other and a ministry to serve the Lord.

Dell came from a loving family where her father and mother demonstrated a great deal of feeling for one another. She expected this from me and often found me cold and undemonstrative. Night after night I lay awake, struggling with this problem. Like many couples, we couldn't discuss these things for years. I'd stare at the ceiling, wondering how a man could express love to his wife in some way other than a sexual experience. Occasionally I would think, *If I wanted to move a load of dirt from one place to another, I'd use a wheelbarrow. But how do you convey this thing called love from one person to another?*

I am convinced that displaying love is learned by experiencing it. As a child, if I had been hugged, caressed, kissed, or touched as an expression of love, it would have been natural for me to express love that way. I had no memory of ever being touched lovingly by anyone. The only touching I had received had been by the end of a belt, board, switch, or a blow struck by the hand. Any caressing or kissing had always been apart from love and done for one's own selfish gratification. I didn't know how to combine the two.

Toward the end of my third year at Emmaus, Chaplain Kosin announced he was leaving to work with Wycliffe Bible Translators. He recommended me to take his place, and in the spring of 1957, I became a full-time chaplain at Cook County Jail. My life's work had begun.

HANDKERCHIEFS

TEN

IN PRE-CIVIL WAR DAYS in Chicago, criminal convicts were housed in the same barns with the horse-drawn streetcars. During the day the prisoners worked on roads and building projects, and the toughest inmate in each barn was put in charge of the group. The name *barn boss* and the system survived the years, and by the time I came to Cook County Jail, the insidious arrangement was as strong as ever. One man on each cellblock was "elected" by his mates, and he kept a tight rein on such things as food distribution, use of mattresses and sheets, as well as passes to visit the chaplain. Shortly after I arrived, Warden Jack Johnson changed *barn boss* to *tier chief,* but that didn't affect the system. Brute force still prevailed.

Many times I had to motivate myself with the Scripture in Luke 9:62, "No man, having put his hand to the plough, and looking back, is fit for the kingdom of God." There were many irksome obstacles. Security regulations kept me from staying in the jail through the two-hour lunch period, so I sat in a nearby park if the weather permitted. If not, I sat in my car. My office was my briefcase. I wasn't allowed to give the inmates any literature directly; anything I distributed had to be sent through the jail mail system.

At 3:00 P.M. I had to leave the jail. But on Fridays they let me back in at 7:00 P.M. to lead a Bible study class.

After several months, the warden decided I could remain inside the jail during lunch in a storage closet on the main floor next to the C block. I thought this was a major step forward and thanked the Lord for progress.

Soon the Bible class went from ten to almost a hundred, the maximum allowed to attend. Many others took Bible correspondence courses, but the difficult restrictions and mail procedures meant great delays and discouragements. Although this seemed like an impossible situation, God had taught me early, through Chaplain Kosin, to take advantage of every opportunity regardless of how small. "Work with the opportunity," Kosin had said. "Learn to face the problems and issues, and pray for strength, wisdom and solutions."

In spite of the barn boss system and peer pressure, scores of men turned to the chaplain for help. I kept a pack of white cards with the name of each man I had talked to and a few notes to remind me of our conversation. Otherwise, going from cellblock to cellblock, I'd forget. So I rotated the cards to keep reminding me of each one.

I felt God had given me a gift, nurtured out of my own youth, to minister to men in jail. To this day it's not hard for me to cut through the elaborate and deceptive stories men devise to con me and get them to open up about their personal lives.

I remember a young man who came to my office dressed as though he'd stepped out of a fashion magazine. He had a silk tie and a handkerchief up his sleeve. He started to cry. His wife was in New Orleans, he told me. He couldn't get in touch with her, and she was worried. Soon he pulled out his little handkerchief and wiped his eyes.

I said, "Well, what are you in here for?"

"Deceptive practices."

"Baloney—you've been running all over the country using stolen credit cards and writing phony checks, haven't you?"

He jumped up. "How do you know that? Did you look at my record?

I said, "No, but what else does a con man do?"

"Nothing."

"What do you want me to call your wife for?" I asked.

"Bond money."

"Why didn't you tell me that? Quit your lying. I would have called." Whether his "worried" wife would do anything, of course, was another matter.

Most of the men in Cook County Jail were from the ghettos on the south and west sides of Chicago. As our evening Bible study grew, I learned more about the restricted, hopeless environment that produced, for example, a Leon and a Gus. They were both part of the group the night we came to Christ's discourse on the Good Shepherd in the Gospel of John. They were having difficulty with John 10:27, where Jesus says, "My sheep hear my voice, and I know them, and they follow me." I doubted that any man in that room had ever seen sheep, and they certainly had difficulty imagining a sheepfold, so I tried to use a word picture more familiar to them.

"What if I came to your apartment building and knocked on the door? There is no glass to look through, and you can't just open the door to anyone. How would you know I was a friend?"

105

They struggled with that for a while, then Leon turned to Gus to try to explain it. They were big men, sitting at one end of a folding table, and Leon kept wagging a finger in Gus's face.

"Well, it's like it says here. I got my sheeps in your sheepfold. I comes in there and call my sheeps, and they just walks right out after me. Your sheeps don't hear my voice, and they stay right there."

He kept on wagging his finger and going over the illustration, when suddenly it became real for Gus. He began to bang on the table and shout.

"Now dis is what I wants to know. What you got your sheeps in my sheepfold for in the first place? Now git 'em out!"

I thought for a moment we'd have a fight on our hands, but we didn't. It pointed out to me, however, the difficulty of communicating spiritual truths to these men.

One night a student in the Bible class cursed God, going on for about ten minutes, accusing God of all kinds of injustice. A few years before, I might have jumped to God's defense, feeling that I had to protect his holiness. This time I tried to listen, to hear what was behind the words.

When he stopped, he looked at me, no doubt expecting me to condemn him. Instead I calmly told him, "I don't believe in the God you described, either. That's not the God of the Bible."

When the session ended that evening, the man prayed, "God, I don't know who you are, but I came down here to find out. Will you please tell me?"

(Another night a student prayed for two men about to be released: "Lord, help these two guys when they get out. Help them to stay out of trouble, and if you can't do that, help them to be slick enough not to get caught.")

I learned in those years that association with convicts could have its hazards as well. One evening Dell and I met with a life insurance salesman. Mr. Rigsby had his charts and literature spread all over our living room, just starting what we were sure would be a lengthy sales pitch, when our doorbell rang. Pushing open the door, I peered into the dimly lighted face of a young man with darting, glazed eyes. He was obviously distraught as he demanded, "Are you Rev. Erwin?"

"Yes, I am. May I help you?"

His unblinking eyes narrowed, "Do you have my handkerchief?"

"Your what?" I asked incredulously.

"My handkerchief. I'm James Green. I gave it to you to keep for me six years ago." Again he asked in a frenzied tone, "Do you have it?" He shifted his weight from one foot to the other.

My mind flew back to my very first jail service six years earlier. This young man had come up to the bars after the service, telling me he was going to the penitentiary to serve his time. He thrust a carefully folded embroidered cotton handkerchief into my hand and asked, "Will you keep this for me until I get out of the joint? It's my girl's."

I had told him I would, and I'd placed the handkerchief in a file folder under his name. But six years had passed, and we had moved three times. For all I could remember, I might have thrown it away. I shuddered at that thought, for this man had a desperation about him that was ominous. Clearly it was the wrong time not to have what he wanted.

As calmly as I could, I told him, "I'll be glad to check for you."

"I'll go turn off my car engine and be right back," he told me, and he scampered down the stairs into the darkness.

When I reentered the living room, Dell and Mr. Rigsby could tell by my ashen face that something was wrong.

"A former inmate is here and wants a handkerchief he gave me to keep six years ago. He's very upset. I can't imagine how he found out where we live. The jail would never give out my address. I hope we can find that handkerchief!"

Mr. Rigsby's eyes grew large. "A former inmate? Out of jail? Here?" Faster than a speeding bullet, he gathered all his charts and told us, "I'll wait outside in my car to see if anything happens." We had discovered a very effective way to get rid of salesmen.

James rang the bell again. When he came into the brighter light, his eyes had a crazed look that really frightened me—all because of a nineteen-cent handkerchief. "Did you find it?" His question sounded more like an ultimatum than a query.

Dell put on a false smile and said, "Won't you come in and sit down?"

"No, I'll stand here till you find it."

Dell continued, "I'm sure we have it in your file; I'll go look."

"How did you find our house, James?" I was curious as well as making a feeble attempt to fill the void with some conversation.

"I asked the jail for your address, but they wouldn't give it to me. They did tell me you lived in Forest Park, though, and I went to the Forest Park police, asking where you lived. They looked up your name in the file they have for vehicle registrations, but wouldn't tell me where you lived. But they did tell me you owned an English Ford. I drove around Forest Park for three hours looking for an English Ford and finally found the one out front and came in."

Dell returned soon, this time with a genuine smile and

108

James's handkerchief in her outstretched hand. It was still neatly folded in the same square as six years ago. I have never appreciated the virtues of a good filing system and an efficient wife more. James jerked the handkerchief from Dell and clutched it to his chest. He choked and sobbed, "That's all I have left of her. She married someone else while I was in the pen." We asked him to stay and talk, but he refused and stumbled out of the house, sobbing convulsively.

Dell and I slumped onto the sofa, overwhelmed with relief and filled with pity for the brokenhearted young man. Suddenly we were startled by the doorbell again. Now what? Was James returning for something else he had given me to keep?

I dragged myself back to the door and switched on the porch light. Never before or since have I been so pleased to see the face of an insurance salesman. "I saw him drive away and wanted to make sure you were all right. I'll contact you in a few days about the insurance."

We never saw James Green again.

A
CRAZY
IDEA

ELEVEN

WE HAD A MAJOR BREAKTHROUGH in 1958 when the warden gave me the jail chapel's broom closet (with brooms removed) to use as an office. I managed to squeeze in a small desk and a file cabinet, and many repentant prisoners committed their lives to God in those cramped quarters.

Eventually I expanded that office. Friends paid for the cement blocks and mortar to build a wall, and the county maintenance crew built it. I now had an inmate clerk and a telephone, and with the help of more friends and an architect, we refurbished the chapel. Christian schools in the city sent students to help us with counseling and Bible classes.

The final steps came when I moved to a larger office and all restrictions were lifted. I had access to any part of the institution day or night. Eight arduous years had passed since I had begun working there full-time. I thought back to the times I had sat in my car in the park and cried, "Lord, what's the sense of going back in there?" It was a rhetorical question. I knew God's answer. He had sent his Son to salvage those men, and the least I could do was tell them about it.

If I hadn't, I often wondered, what might have happened to a man like Peter Cherevchenko? Peter was an enormous Russian, a bear of a man who intimidated most prisoners with his broken English and powerful frame.

One day he found an inmate praying in his cell and yelled at him, "You pray? You teach me to pray!"

As a boy in Russia in the thirties, he had been forbidden to learn about God. He was captured by the Germans as they retreated from Russia in 1943 and forced to work in a concentration camp. He knew hunger and deprivation, and when the Americans liberated the prisoners, he and his father came to the United States. Stalin was sentencing war prisoners to slave labor camps in Siberia, and this meant he had to leave his mother, sister, and brother behind. He never saw them again.

In this country his temper, which matched his huge fists, got him into too many barroom brawls, and he landed in Cook County Jail.

The prisoner whom Peter found praying told him he should come to see me, so Peter got a pass to go to church service in the chapel. There, he told me later, "I heard a beautiful song I'd never heard before," and reverently he pronounced each word, "What a Friend We Have in Jesus."

Because English was difficult for him then, I found a minister who spoke Russian, and after several counseling sessions Peter committed his life to Christ. The inmates on his cellblock noticed the change almost immediately. "What happened to Pete?" they'd ask. "He's not mean anymore."

Released from jail, he went back to the taverns and his

114

old life, but one Sunday morning as he sat staring into a drink, he began to pound on the bar and yell, "My God, what am I doing here? I should be in church." With his new wife, Sonia, he began to attend a Russian church, where his faith grew. When I see Peter now and then, he hugs me warmly with huge arms, and as I struggle for breath, he tells me, "I never forget what Johnny do for me."

During those years, I believe God was preparing me for something far ahead. I have some idea now why he had Moses and the apostle Paul spend the years in the desert, learning his ways, before he called them to the greatest mission of their lives.

I was learning in my relationship with Dell as well. We had no one to explain to us that the battered years of my youth could severely hinder our growth together. Dell yearned for a baby, but I stalled her as long as I could, never daring to tell her of my fears in having children. Not only did I fear being unable to love them, but I was terrified to think about the possibility of dying, as my father had, and leaving a child to grow up the way I did. It seemed better never to have a child than to put one on the same sorrowful path I had followed.

Finally I gave in, secretly hoping that one of us was sterile. Then Dell became pregnant, and when ten-pound, four-and-a-half ounce Vance David (for David Pitman) arrived, there wasn't a prouder father alive. I was amazed and overwhelmed at the love I felt for him, and few men have prayed as I did that God would give me the grace and understanding a father needed. Four years later I overcame my fears of being unable to love additional children when our twins, Gregg Robert and Gayle Rozzie (for Rozzie Pitman) were born.

By this time we were into the incredible 1960s, the decade in which the discontent of American blacks

115

spilled into the streets while Viet Nam spawned violent riots and the cities burned. The unrest on the outside was reflected in life behind bars. Inmates brought the problems of the street in with them, and news from the outside triggered a response.

Early in 1967 President Johnson opened a massive attack on crime in response to pressure from the cities. Washington had heard in no uncertain terms that urban problems were as important as Viet Nam, and in a moment of frustration, LBJ remarked, "Things could be worse; I could be a mayor."

I noticed that the age level of the jail population was rapidly decreasing, along with the educational ability of the prisoners. I dealt less and less with the professional burglar or con man and more with young frustrated black from Chicago's South and West Side ghettos.

For years I had sent men back into society with the admonition, "Now work hard. Get a good job, or go back to school. Stay out of trouble. Find good friends." Then I added, "Trust and obey the Lord, and he'll keep you out of jail." I should have known from my own experience that all the will power in the world can't always overcome the traps of a man's environment. But I hadn't lived in the ghetto. I sensed only vaguely that decent employment requires training, that the present methods of instruction weren't educating these men, their housing was uninhabitable, and the present welfare systems only perpetuated crime and poverty.

I also noticed more and more that when I asked a man to read a verse of Scripture, he couldn't. One of my favorite passages was in 1 John 5, where it says, "He that hath the Son hath life." A man might get the first few words, but instead of "hath" he would read "hates." I'd use John 3:16 quite often and found that many men stumbled on such simple words as "son." Then I knew I had a long, tough job ahead to take them verbally through the spiritual concepts, and even when I was finished, they were still dependent on me. They couldn't read and learn more for themselves.

Slowly it dawned on me that not only were they unable to read, but they had no job skills, work habits, or experience. They couldn't even fill out an application to get a job.

But that wasn't my responsibility. Employment . . . education . . . they were secular. My call was to reach the souls of men, I reminded myself. Then I would go home at night and lie awake while memories of my own life flashed by. I could hear Judge Kay telling me, "You can't succeed in life without a high-school education." (Then he sent me to an institution where I couldn't get one.) What good would my "blessing" do these men? A good dose of literacy so they could read the Word themselves would be a lot better.

My attitude, I knew, was condemned by the Bible where it says, "If you have a friend who is in need of food and clothing, and you say to him, 'Well, good-bye and God bless you; stay warm and eat hearty,' and then don't give him clothes or food, what good does that do?" (James 2:15-16, Living Bible).

A long corridor connects the Cook County Courthouse to the jail, and the inmates who have walked it call it the "Boulevard of Broken Dreams." Many times I'd see men coming back down this hall after I'd counseled with them and waved farewell several weeks before, and they'd be wearing the same hopeless expression they had worn when I first met them. My stomach would knot with both sympathy and guilt, but I'd overcome these feelings by saying, "Well, that man didn't really get converted. He wasn't really sincere. After all, don't the Scriptures say that by their fruits you shall know them, and that the dog returns to his vomit and the hog to wallowing in the mire?"

Of course I misinterpreted these verses and ignored the verses that applied to me. I was a master at interpreting Scripture for others but not in applying practical verses to myself. Quickly I would shift my thoughts to how I could really get this man converted this time and pray for God to remove the scales from his eyes and help him to see his insincerity.

Eventually I could no longer silence my conscience with misapplied Scriptures, and a wrestling match took place inside. Half of me wanted to help the inmates in all areas of their needs, while the other half told me to beware of a social gospel and of leaving my spiritual ministry. This tug of war was so intense that at times I felt like a split personality. My past experiences took on more meaning. I remembered how God had touched my life so many times through people—a social worker, Amos, my fellow workers in Greenfield, Dave and Rozzie, and my friends in Augusta all marched through my mind as God's instruments in my life. I could identify God's working through all of them and many others, giving me bits of sustenance at times when I was starving emotionally, when I was sure God was absent from my life.

Finally some new insights broke through. I had read Jesus' words, when he quoted an Old Testament Scripture. ". . . Man shall not live by bread alone, but by every word that proceedeth out of the mouth of God" (Matthew 4:4). I had been conscious only of the latter part. I had ignored the fact that man must live by bread. Of course he must have his physical needs met, and that included education and a job. I became convinced that I should try to teach a few men to read and help them get jobs, at least the ones I was counseling. That's all I planned to do.

My first idea, since I never imagined anything could be done inside the jail, was to use a vacant floor at the Pacific Garden Mission over on South State Street as a school for ex-offenders I had counseled. I asked to speak to their board of directors, carefully planning my presentation and outlining what I thought was the Christian's responsibility. All I wanted to do was to teach a few men to read.

They were polite, asked a few questions, but it all seemed vague to them. No one appeared interested, and I left discouraged. These men were wise, respected, experienced Christians. They knew God's will. My crazy idea must be just that—a crazy idea.

Two days later I got a call from one of the businessmen who had been at the board meeting. Lorne Renner was a gray-flannel-suit type, with well-shined shoes and closely cropped graying hair, articulate, a man of action as well as ideas. I was impressed.

"I heard what you had to say, John. l think you've got something there, and I'd like to help."

I had no idea what he meant, but we made an appointment for the next day at the jail, where he could get more than a boardroom feel for the problem. Lorne, it turned out, had a friend at Illinois Institute of Technology who designed programs to educate the hard-core unemployed. He called his friend, and in a shorter time than I would have imagined, we had a small experimental program going.

With Lorne's help I began to find my way around a new world for me outside of the prison. We approached the Bell & Howell company, and they agreed to loan us some language masters, audio-visual machines that teach reading. We heard of an innovative education program at a jail in Alabama and made a trip there to study it.

As far as we knew, all educational programs for inmates were in penitentiaries, where the sentences are

119

long-term. At Cook County Jail, most of the men are waiting trial or transfer to the penitentiary, and the sentence for those convicted only runs from one day to a year. We hoped to prove that something could be done in a short period of time to improve a person's ability to get a job and adjust to society. And, of course, if he could read a job application, he could begin to read the Word of God. I wouldn't separate the two in my mind.

My clerk Don was one of the first prisoners we put into our pilot program. I called him into my office.

"We've got these machines here, Don, and I want you to help us try them out."

I put ten words that Don couldn't read on the language master and gave him instructions. They were simple words—*cat, hat, ball, bat.* The machine works on a programmed self-learning system. As soon as a man learns something, he goes on to the next step. He's encouraged by learning in bite-sized portions and seeing immediate progress.

I went back to work in my office behind the chapel, and about thirty minutes later I heard a pecking noise on the window. I looked up and saw Don grinning from ear to ear. He had learned all ten words and was not only surprised he could learn but was hungry for more. Most important, he'd learned that he could learn. The years of thinking he was dumb, of teachers' and parents' disparaging comments, of believing he was a failure had begun to fade with that simple experiment. A new world was unfolding, not only for Don but for hundreds of other young men in the same hopeless situation.

THE SHERIFF AND THE SENATOR

TWELVE

WITH OTHER PRISONERS WE LEARNED that over a period of several months we could raise the reading level of a man about one grade per month of study. Don actually reached a fifth-grade level in five weeks. By that time the IIT researchers had some data for their theses, and we had some hard evidence to present to the world.

I wondered at the same time if we had gone a step too far without some kind of official permission. To keep the program moving, we had incorporated it and called it PACE—Programmed Activities for Correctional Education. We planned to apply to foundations for money to hire staff and get more machines, but first we needed the sanction of the powers that be.

The sheriff's office oversees the correctional facilities of Cook County, and Sheriff Richard Ogilvie had stopped by my office many times, asking questions, trying to learn more about the jail and its inmates.

Initially, I hadn't had much regard for politicians. My

conservative brand of religion for the past dozen years had taught me they were all alike—self-serving men, dishonest. I did my duty by praying for them, but I certainly didn't have to associate with them.

When Richard Ogilvie stopped by to ask about the weather, I wished to myself he'd call the weather bureau. I had important work to do—God's work. I had to admit he didn't fit my stereotype of the cigar-smoking, back-slapping sheriff, but I wasn't going to be fooled by that. They were all alike underneath.

When he had asked me to give the invocation at a graduation ceremony for sheriff's police, I'd hesitated. Again, my church world had taught me that *invocation* was a modernist expression used by liberals, and I wanted nothing to do with it. Some streak of common sense in me, however, told me that what he really wanted me to do was to pray, to ask God to bless these men. They could call it an invocation if they wanted, but I recognized it as an opportunity to share God's love and concern with some men beyond the confines of the jail, so I agreed to go.

It had been raining the morning of the ceremony, and as I drove the wet streets of Chicago, I felt a twinge of nervousness at standing before the county officials. Several blocks before the expressway, I entered an intersection at the same time that I caught sight of a red flash in the corner of my eye. Suddenly I was jolted, and my car spun around and rammed a massive elm on the parkway. I sat there stunned for a moment until I heard screaming, and a short, dark man with a turban came running towards me, yelling in a dialect I couldn't understand, and waving his arms. I hoped the turban meant he was the follower of some nonviolent religion, because I had to explain to him that he had driven his brand-new Ford Falcon through a stop sign into my Oldsmobile F-85.

And I had to do it quickly if I were to get to the graduation ceremony.

Leaving the little man in the rain, I walked to a nearby house and called the sheriff's police, and in a short time they dispatched a squad car to pick me up. Now, I wondered, was God trying to tell me something? Perhaps I had misread his will, and this idea of praying at a government ceremony was a bad idea after all. But I went ahead, and it seemed to me that Sheriff Ogilvie was thankful for the simple prayer offered that day.

That incident flashed through my mind as I entered the Civic Center one August morning in 1967 and rode the elevator to the seventh-floor office of the sheriff. I had come to tell him about PACE and ask for his approval. We had begun to envision larger things by this time, but without his endorsement, we'd get nowhere.

The sheriff's office at that time had two large windows facing west, and Ogilvie sat with his back toward them looking at me. While he was cordial, there was nothing in his greeting to encourage me. Just a "Yes," as if to say, "I have ten minutes I've blocked off for you, now say your piece."

I plunged in, told him about PACE and Don and the IIT people and Lorne Renner and our plans. I explained that Warden Johnson had encouraged us to apply for federal funds through the Department of Labor, and I needed to go to Washington to get the approval of Illinois congressmen. I hardly knew where Washington was, much less who might help me there.

That day I received Richard Ogilvie's complete support, and several months later, when he had become president of the county board, he picked up his telephone while I sat in his office and called Senator Charles Percy. "Percy's the man you need to see," he explained, but Percy was out, so Ogilvie promised he would mention

125

my need to him in a few days.

Another forgotten promise, I thought. *He has more to do than put in a good word to a senator for a chaplain.* I left discouraged. A few days later I received a letter from Senator Percy inviting me to Washington. In the midst of my excitement, I mentally apologized to Ogilvie for my lack of trust, then rushed home that night to prepare.

I had never been to Washington, and I knew nothing of the workings of government. Somewhat frightened, I arrived in the senator's office, an insignificant chaplain, a former welfare kid, about to meet some of the nation's most powerful people. Percy was open and warm, and to my relief, he quickly grasped the concepts of the program. I had done enough homework to know that the Department of Labor had funds available through the Manpower Development and Training Act, and I asked for his help in making contacts. Within ten minutes I had five appointments.

The next step wasn't so easy. Labor Department officials suggested I go back to Chicago and work through the local offices of the Illinois State Employment Service. If I could present a convincing proposal using their guidelines, perhaps—no promises, you understand—I could get a grant. Having no idea of all that faced me in the next year, I eagerly returned to Chicago to start on the proposal.

Some months before we began the PACE experiment, I had received a letter addressed simply to "Protestant Chaplain" from a Joel Ayres, a college student interested in becoming a prison chaplain and seeking advice. I invited him to spend a day with me at the jail, and when he came, I sensed he was lonely, empty, and searching for an answer to his own life, as I had been years before.

Most of the day I tried to convert him, but my techniques failed to produce anything except a great deal of frustration that I couldn't get the response I wanted from him. He just stared with wonder while I preached at him, and I couldn't imagine what was going through his mind.

At the end of the day, I gave up and invited him to attend the meeting of the chaplains' association in the spring, never expecting to see him again. But it didn't matter. I had, I thought, thoroughly evangelized him, and now he was responsible for his own soul.

That spring of '67 Joel surprised me by attending the chaplains' meeting. But afterwards he turned and sadly told me, "I don't want to be a prison chaplain anymore. I have nothing to offer the men."

By now I was slowly forming a new opinion about conversion. I was becoming convinced that if this man or anyone were ever converted, God would have to do it. I decided not to give him my simple steps-to-the-Savior plan, backed by my carefully chosen Scripture verses. All I said was "Well, perhaps we should discuss your life. If you want to, telephone me when you get out of school for the summer." I was through manipulating people into professions of faith.

To my surprise, Joel called me in June and asked to see me. This time I suggested we take a walk, and we crossed California Avenue to the nearby park. I began telling him my own story, what I found to make my life meaningful, using every illustration and metaphor I knew. He kept indicating that I should go on, and after nearly two hours of one-sided conversation, I ran out of words. I said, "Joel, I don't know anything else to tell you. Have you ever accepted Christ as your Savior?"

"Yes."

"When?" I asked incredulously.

"While you were talking."

127

My first impulse was to kick him off the cement pillar on which he was perched and say, "Why didn't you save me all this effort?!" I didn't know his side of the story until later. When he had returned to college after his first visit to the jail, he thought nothing really significant had happened until it struck him—*why, this busy, involved man let me spend a whole day with him, watching him work—a whole day, and I'm just a nobody.*

Now he had listened for two hours, never having heard God or Christ or the Bible explained that way before. "I didn't want you to stop talking," he told me. "It was not only what you said, but who you were during that time. You cared enough about me to give me two hours of your undivided attention. In my entire life no one had ever spent two continuous hours with me. I had always been average, and nobody spends time with an average kid."

God had become real to Joel Ayres because I had thought enough of him to spend a little time with him. His story was so much like mine. For both of us, the reality of God rested in real people who demonstrated love to us with no strings attached. I had read verses about that in the Bible many times: ". . . our very lives were further proof to you of the truth of our message. So you became our followers and the Lord's" (1 Thess. 1:5-6, Living Bible). Now I understood what those Scriptures meant.

Soon after that Joel joined the small group of PACE volunteers, helping us set up the machines, counsel the prisoners, run the tests, and administer the program. Word had spread, and we had more requests than we could handle—but no money. With some fear and, I confess, little faith, we presented our need to the Sears Roebuck Foundation. We had to do something to keep alive until we heard from Washington. Sears granted us

$5,000, and we hired Joel for $50 a week, our first employee.

We knocked on a few more doors, but most people were skeptical. I was only a chaplain, and what good could come out of Cook County Jail, anyhow? Encouraged by the help from Sears, we went back and worked on our proposal for Washington. With no place else to work, we set up a small office in our home with a typewriter in our bathroom. IBM, we concluded, meant International Bathroom Machinery, and we spent long hours typing our carefully prepared document. Finally it was ready, and I boarded a plane a second time for Washington with our precious proposal under my arm.

UPWARD
IN THE
NIGHT

THIRTEEN

AT THE SAME TIME our fledgling program was helping a handful of prisoners, the wrath of the press and various citizens' groups burst on Warden Johnson and his administration. The national news media, as well as those in Chicago, ran feature stories on the corruption and mismanagement of Cook County Jail, and a grand jury began an investigation. Soon our jail became known as the most corrupt institution in America.

So when I sat down with Labor Department officials to present our program and request, I could feel the hostility in the air. I was the man from Chicago. Did I really expect them to put good government money into that filthy place?

They had brought advisers to the meeting—an educator, a sociologist, and some others. Each was a specialist in something, and I had had my fill of specialists. It probably showed.

It wasn't a very successful meeting. "Go back to

Chicago," they told me. "Clean up your jail first."

I can't say that they had no reason for their suspicions. What they couldn't seem to understand, however, was that I had nothing to do with running the jail. I'm not paid by the county. The very program I set before them came about because the jail system wasn't working. It was designed to relieve some of the ills of the system. I felt it was unfair to be held accountable for something I had no responsibility for, but I had to admit I might have felt that way myself in their place.

Discouraged, I went back to Chicago to await the official answer to our request, and I headed into a storm that threatened many times to sweep me away It shouldn't have surprised me. The Bible warns us ᵗo ᵉxpect persecution, but I wasn't prepared for this.

First came a group of professionals—a sociologist, a psychologist, and a penologist who had spent thousands of dollars and man-hours on studies and concluded that we couldn't do what we were doing. We were only religionists, not educators, and naive to boot. What did we know about changing behavior? I thought these people who had spent years looking for a way to help inmates would be delighted with our program. Instead, I was accused of falsifying statistics, not operating scientifically, and even misappropriating funds.

A group of social agencies—Red Feather, Salvation Army, and some others—asked me to speak at one of their meetings about what we were doing. I followed a professor who had just finished a study costing some thousands and concluding that it would take millions of dollars to do anything effective at Cook County Jail. I didn't ask for that spot on the program, but when I stood up and told about the prisoners who had raised their reading level three or four or five grades in as many months, it only increased the scorn he heaped on me.

But when the Christians opened fire, they nearly wiped me out. For all my years of ministry, I had depended on the support of Christian people for my salary as well as for invaluable counsel, vital prayer backing, and encouragement. When they started to question our work, they came on strong. Some hinted they'd cut off our financial support; others did so without a word. Some accused us of "leaving our calling" or "preaching a social gospel" or "departing from the faith."

Only one accuser ever came to talk with us. She left convinced we were still committed to serving the Lord. But others chose to hold special prayer meetings for our restoration.

The storm had plenty of wind left in it, and by September, 1968, we still had no word from Washington. Chicago had just reeled through riots of that year's Democratic Convention, and the election campaign and the war was sapping the energy of many government leaders. I figured they had little time to give away money. But our funds were just about depleted, and the critics, each claiming to know the will of God for us, kept up their screaming. (Ironically, God seemed to have given each one a different plan.)

Early that month I met with a foundation to request funds to continue PACE, and they turned us down. I went back to the jail that afternoon as low as I could get. My next appointment was to talk to a man sentenced to the electric chair. I felt like following him. When he left my office, I began to pray, but not one of those flowery "prayer meeting" prayers. I simply said, "God, I quit. I've had it. I don't have the backbone or the will to continue. I'm tired of listening to all these people, when you're the only one who knows what I should do. Unless you assure me today that I'm in your will, I'm finished. I'm simply too weak to continue."

On my desk was a calendar with a verse of Scripture and a few lines of inspirational poetry for each day. I glanced at it for that day and read, "Seest thou a man diligent in his business? he shall stand before kings" (Prov. 22:29).* Then it went on, "Do today's work well, however lowly; perhaps tomorrow God will have something larger for you." The reading ended:

The heights by great men reached and kept
Were not attained by sudden flight;
But they, while their companions slept,
Were toiling upward in the night.

I read it again: "Do today's work well . . . toiling upward in the night." If ever God had a message for me at the right time in the right place, that was it. I'm sure I've missed what he's tried to say to me many times, but I couldn't miss it that day in my jail office. I made a covenant then with God that I would stick with PACE until every door on earth closed and it was impossible to go on, or until PACE became a reality. I asked only that he would go with me and give me the courage and strength.

With that, the depression lifted. I had peace for the first time in weeks, and I knew in my heart our experiment would blossom.

Many doors did close after that. The tide of events did not suddenly turn. The critics didn't let up, nor did the money come rolling in. But I had the will and the strength to wait and bear with it.

The money especially was a problem. I could learn to live with the critics, but when the last dime went out, we couldn't carry on. I went back to Washington and once

---

*This scripture seemed to be remarkably fulfilled in September, 1976, when I was asked to give the invocation at one of President Ford's political dinners.

136

again made the rounds to Congressman Rostenkowski, Congressman Rumsfeld, Congressman Pucinski. They all wanted to help. None, of course, could make the final decision.

A new Catholic chaplain, Father Joseph McDonnell, had been assigned to the jail about that time, a priest with deep commitments to God and the inmates. We shared many problems together, and I said to him one day, "Father Mac, we haven't heard a word about our proposal. Let's see if we can get the newspaper on our side." Having put my foot out that far, I had to follow through, and I called the *Chicago Tribune* and asked for the editor, Clayton Kirkpatrick.

He agreed to see us, so we made an appointment for October 8 at 4:00 P.M. I'm convinced that where the Bible says, "Ye have not, because ye ask not," it applies to asking help from people as well as from God. So Father Mac and I put our program before the editor and sat back as if to say, "Now what can you do for us?"

I wondered, however, if we had talked too much, if our boldness would offend this highly respected newspaperman. He had listened quietly with only a few questions, but now he smiled at us and said, "Gentlemen, I think you've got something we're interested in. I'll not only have a reporter do a story on your work, but I'll have a correspondent in Washington cover you when you go there again."

We left downtown Chicago in the middle of the evening rush hour and a sudden downpour. The rain stalled traffic, but we had some cause for hope as we inched our way back to the jail. I no sooner had my coat off than the phone in my office rang. It was the warden to tell me that a reporter was in his office preparing a story on PACE. The story ran a few days later and, true to his word, the next time I went to Washington, the *Tribune* ran another piece on our fight to get support for PACE.

Meanwhile, God had more work to do in my life. I had begun to realize in the past year or so that I wore religious blinders that kept me from looking too far to the left or right. God certainly couldn't use anyone who walked outside my line of vision.

That's why I had some reservations when a friend suggested I invite Dr. Clarence Jordan to speak at a chaplains' meeting. I'd been active for some time in the American Correctional Chaplains' Association and had set up displays offering Bibles and correspondence courses for other chaplains to use in their ministry. When those whom I had tagged as "outside" my circle of Christianity had picked up these materials and expressed thanks for them, I had some head scratching to do. Now I asked for a tape recording of Dr. Jordan so I could hear this man before I invited him. Actually, I wanted to check him out, to put my stamp of approval on him, to pronounce him "clean" before we invited him.

I took the tape home and sat back one evening to listen. Dr. Jordan was preaching on the humanity of Jesus, and he unveiled the Lord as a man who really felt what people felt, suffered emotionally even as I did, and was tempted the same way. He ate real food; he cried, he laughed, he cared as a man. His greatest judgments and rebukes, moreover, were for those who isolated themselves from human involvement. He denounced the self-righteous and the religious who couldn't feel the hurt, the fears, and the needs of their fellow men.

As Dr. Jordan used the Beatitudes for a text, I realized I had often been guilty. I had isolated myself from many of God's servants, from many men who cared deeply. I had a new appreciation for the humanity of Jesus and what it really meant, and I would need that for the struggle ahead.

While we had incorporated PACE and had a board of directors, funds were channeled through the local school board. After all, it was an educational program, and they were responsible for education in the jail. So I suppose it was understandable they'd want to control it. But they couldn't seem to understand why I should have anything to say about it. I was just a chaplain. What did I know about education? Why didn't I go and counsel all those prisoners and, of course, raise the money in my spare time to keep PACE alive?

I almost did that. At times I almost gave up and turned the entire program over to them—except that I felt strongly about several things. The program simply wouldn't work if controlled by public educators. If we couldn't choose our own people and set our own goals, PACE was doomed. I was also convinced that God had led me to create PACE and that if it did get bogged down, the inmates would be the ones to lose. So I hung on.

Driving home from the jail one night after a stormy day of charges and innuendos, ploys and counterploys, I heard a tune on the radio that stuck in my mind. Music, more than anything else, captivates me and moves me. I could be sitting in the most important meeting of my life, and if someone turned on music, I'd silently follow the intricacies of the orchestra rather than concentrate on the speaker. When the deejay played a song from the movie *Camelot*, I knew I had to see the film.

That night I checked the paper and found *Camelot* playing at the Meadowbrook Cinema not far from our house. It was a Tuesday, and not more than a score of people were there as Dell and I watched the story unfold.

Camelot, to refresh your memory, is the eternal-triangle story of King Arthur, his wife Guinevere, and his best friend, Lancelot. King Arthur knew that Guinevere loved and was loved by Lancelot, and that these two unfaithful friends were about to bring his idyllic kingdom to an end.

As I watched, I identified in anguish with King Arthur, because I felt that those who ought to be my friends were betraying me and helping disrupt PACE. And as King Arthur forgave them both and kept loving them, I knew God was speaking to me in that theater, "Forgive and go on, John."

Finally, in August, 1969, we heard from the Department of Labor. They agreed to fund the program for $200,000 for one year—if we could start a building within six months. They couldn't tie the funds up any longer.

Six months? A building would cost at least seventy-five to a hundred thousand dollars. How could we ever get the money and start a building in that time?

But even more importantly, where would we put it? We didn't own any land.

For years I had noticed a piece of ground 50 by 150 feet between two of the cellblocks and had envisioned a building there. But people would think I was crazy to even suggest such a thing. Who ever heard of building your own building inside a jail compound, especially Cook County Jail?

As we prayed about it, I remembered again the verse, "Ye have not, because ye ask not." Well, we could ask God, but we'd also have to ask Richard Ogilvie's successor, Sheriff Woods. So, summoning my courage, I put the strange request before him, and, to my surprise, he agreed.

I also learned that Inland-Ryerson Steel Company made buildings suitable for any purpose, so I went to their foundation asking for help.

"What size building do you need?" they asked.

"Forty by 150 feet."

"Who told you?"

"Who told me what?"

They explained that forty feet was the standard width of their buildings, which they sold by the foot. They not only agreed to sell us one at cost but to help us substantially from their foundation.

Now Joel and I scurried around frantically to every Chicago area corporation, foundation, church, and individual we could who we thought might help. We learned that a state agency would match the private funds we raised. We needed $88,000 altogether.

Slowly the money came in and we began to build, keeping one eye on the six-month deadline. Joel and I were working long hours now, but we weren't done yet. We had to do much of the inside work ourselves to save money. Between the time the bids went out and construction began, costs had risen some $30,000. That was when we received the greatest encouragement we'd had in a long time.

Volunteers came from all over the city to help us each night. Executives from top Chicago corporations put on their overalls in the evening and got on their knees beside laborers, clerks, salespeople, and inmates to lay tile and bend conduit and paint walls. And when the deadline came, we had a building ready.

Some people had told me that to get government funds, I'd have to compromise some ethical principles or sell my political soul. Not so. In all my dealings with the government, no one has ever hinted that I do anything dishonest; no one has ever asked me to sacrifice any principle; and no one has put his hand out behind him. As long as we've complied with the guidelines of the grant, we've had no problems.

Up to this time all we had done was teach men to read. We didn't have space in the chapel for anything else. I

141

knew that a lot more was needed, however. When Don, my clerk with whom we had begun the pilot program, had been released, I had telephoned a friend who owned a printing company in downtown Chicago. "Send Don down," he told me, "and I'll find a job for him."

I gave Don the address, satisfied that I had helped him spiritually and also by teaching him to read and get a job. Now I was reaching the whole man.

A few days later I called my printer friend to see how Don was doing. A disappointed voice said, "He didn't ever show up." I mumbled some apology on Don's behalf and hung up in disgust. All the time and help I had given him—and he didn't even care enough to go four miles for a job interview.

I was angry as I drove out to Chicago's West Side and found Don in front of his apartment building, sitting on a crumbly step, baloney sandwich in one hand, beer in the other. I asked him to get in my car where we could talk privately, and then I began to berate him.

"So you didn't even have the decency to show up for the job after all the time and trouble I've taken for you! You wasted my time; you wasted the volunteer's time. You really don't want to work. You want to be a bum all your life, don't you?"

He washed down his sandwich with a slug of beer before he spoke. Haltingly, eyes downcast, he said, "Chaplain . . . I don't know where that printing place was at. I ain't never been downtown, and I'm afraid to go."

I apologized to him, and then I taught him how to get on which bus, where to go. But more importantly, I learned that the men in Cook County Jail needed more than a few reading lessons. They needed to learn how to live on the outside. They needed work skills and social skills, and they needed a friend, a counselor, someone to guide them through the maze of cultural traps that would land them back in jail. We needed a comprehensive program.

And now we had the space to create it. The Manpower Development and Training Act had called for an expansion of experimental job training programs for prisoners, so our grant included funds for vocational training, counseling, and follow-up services as well. We could also pay each inmate fifteen dollars a week for spending most of his day learning.

On February 27, 1970, we held a teary, emotional dedication ceremony in our completed building between the cellblocks. Classes began immediately with sixty students.

STAYING CLEAN

FOURTEEN

As MORE MEN ENROLLED in PACE, we needed help, so we hired educators and teachers, clerks and counselors. However, we needed people with skills that can't be learned in school, a love and concern for inmates that can't be described in a job application. God sent some unusual people, but the story that thrills me perhaps more than any other is that of Richard Russell.

A drug addict who had been in and out of jail, including Cook County, dozens of times, Richard was just finishing five years at Menard State Penitentiary in 1964. He was "clean," five years without drugs; he had a new suit on his back and twenty-five dollars in his pocket as he stepped on the bus for Chicago.

Now, however, the old feeling began to come back. His nose ran a little, his eyes watered, and a queasy sensation gripped his stomach. There shouldn't be any withdrawal symptoms now—but there they were, reminding him that being free wasn't all it was cracked up to be.

Once in the city, Richard found the nearest phone booth and dialed a familiar number.

"What's happening, man? Got anything?"

"Aw, man, where you been?"

"I just got back."

"Man, stay clean."

"I don't want no preaching. You got any stuff?"

"Yeah, I got stuff."

"Well, I'll be right over. I'm not gonna get hooked. I just wanna little bit to stop this nose from running. I'm not gonna use no more stuff."

But as soon as the needle pierced his vein, he was hooked again.

For twenty years Richard Russell's life had been one continuous cycle of drugs, thefts, jail, and back around again. Only the rest and recuperation he got in jail helped his body survive the torture he inflicted on it while out. When an addict has a "long run" (a lengthy period without arrest), his body demands larger and larger doses and progressively deteriorates. Getting jailed is a blessing that keeps him alive.

Richard had also been in and out of drug treatment centers, including stays at the federal hospital in Lexington, Kentucky, but went right back to stealing autos, robbing liquor stores, and burglarizing homes to get money for drugs once he was out. He did his time at Menard for forging checks.

Like so many Cook County Jail inmates, Richard was a product of the streets of Chicago. As a kid he spent part of his time in Georgia living with his father and part in Chicago with his mother. He loved them both, but at twelve he made his own decision to stay in Chicago in his mother's apartment in the Cottage Grove area.

He joined the Four Corners gang in the forties when fists, not zip guns or chains, were the chief weapons.

Wine, however, was as common as Pepsi among his friends, and they spent more time smoking reefers and shooting dice than studying reading, writing, and arithmetic.

At seventeen he joined the Marines, fought in the Far East, then returned to his old haunts. One night at a party, a girlfriend took him to a corner of the room and gave him a dab of white powder to sniff. It was cocaine, and although he found it bitter, it gave him the high he wanted. Several weeks later he found blood on his pillow, and a friend told him that snorting coke would cause nose cancer.

The "friend" then showed him how to shoot heroin. He shook a little of the drug into a wine bottle cap, added a few drops of water, and heated it with a match until the powder dissolved. Then shaking the cap until it cooled, he took a tiny wad of cotton from the lining of the tongue of his shoe, balled it up, and dropped it in the cap. This served as a strainer through which he drew the liquid into a syringe. Next he tightened his belt around Richard's forearm until his veins popped, and he plunged the needle in.

Soon he was up to a hundred-dollar-a-day habit. He had learned to play the drums and worked as a jazz drummer, but his drums spent more time in pawn shops, and he had to steal even more to get them out.

It was years later, on a hot summer evening in 1964, just about sunset, that Richard and a friend walked down Forty-fourth Street in Chicago on their way to a shooting gallery (a place where they could get the needle and equipment). Both men had two small plastic bags of heroin on them when a police car pulled up. Normally Richard would have swallowed the drug to destroy the evidence, but this time he was already high and his mind was foggy. With his hand down by his leg, he flicked the

149

bags away, but it didn't take the officers long to find them.

Back in Cook County Jail, Richard met an old friend, Willie McCoy, and they began talking about their mothers, who attended church regularly, and how they prayed for their sons. Both hoped to get out of jail because of their mothers' prayers.

During supper one night, Willie swallowed a mouthful of beans, dropped his spoon on the metal plate, and said, "You know what, man? We should stop shuckin' and jivin' and kiddin' ourselves."

"Yeah, man, you right."

"There's a man here named Chaplain Erwin. I'm gonna see him, and you oughta see him, too."

"See him? F' what?" Richard asked.

"To get something on your mind, man, get saved. I hear he is really a man of God."

"You kidding! In here?" Richard was sure that any minister connected with any jail or any part of the system had to be phony. Suspicious and doubting, but sick of the mess he had made of his life, he wanted a way out, any way. At thirty-seven he was sick and tired of drugs, of stealing, of running from the police. He was weary of the misery of needing a fix so badly he could kill for it and weary of the panic in the streets from police interference that had scared off the pushers. During those times he might have had enough money, but couldn't find a place to score, and the indescribably awful withdrawal symptoms would begin as every nerve and joint screamed in pain for the narcotic. His stomach would thrash wildly, waves of nausea sweeping over him, and he would contort with dry heaves. Cramps would bend him double with excruciating pains. At times he was afraid he was going to die, and at times he was afraid he was not going to die.

He had seen friends die from drugs. Butterball, for example, was chubby when he first shot heroin, but soon he became as emaciated as all addicts. One night Richard and Butterball were in a shooting gallery, and after Butterball took his injection, he drifted into a stupor. Richard took the needle from his arm, washed it out with water, used it, and passed it around. Noticing that Butterball was still unconscious and aware something must be wrong, they walked him around. When he failed to respond, they put him in a tub of cold water, but he never roused. He was dead. There was nothing else they could do. They carried him to an abandoned car and left him, afraid they might get arrested for his death.

Once he had watched a friend die of a "hot shot," a special dose prepared for Brother Holmes, who was a stool pigeon. A "hot shot" was either heroin mixed with strychnine or else pure heroin, strong enough to kill. As soon as the needle pricked Brother Holmes's vein, he screamed, and it was all over.

It was with these memories that Richard Russell first came to see me.

"I'll give you some toothpaste, soap, and stationery, and you can make one phone call," I began routinely.

"I don't have no one to call, chaplain." He explained that everyone he knew had given up on him long ago.

Still trying to stay a step ahead, I told him I would not go to a judge to try to help. Many of the inmates at Cook County are waiting for trial and think that a word from the chaplain will turn the key.

Richard went on, however, to tell me his life's story, concluding that he wanted to get straight with God. I suggested we get down on our knees and pray, and the two of us knelt there in my cramped quarters at the back of the jail chapel.

Silently he waited for me to pray, but I told him, "You

151

want to give your life to the Lord? Tell him about it. Just talk to him like you talked to me."

So Richard began, "Lord, help me. Have mercy on me. . . ." And on he went, asking God to forgive him and make him a new man. That was September 16, 1964.

Richard returned to his cellblock, and he and Willie McCoy began a prayer meeting. Willie was the barn boss, a two-time loser, convicted twice for armed robbery and now arrested again on the same charge. He was in danger of being sentenced as a habitual criminal.

While some of the inmates secretly derided the prayer group, they didn't dare say anything directly to Willie or Richard, and the group grew. The word spread around the jail, and Richard came often to see me and enrolled in a Bible study correspondence course.

He was still worried, however, that once outside he'd go back to his old life. And, of course, he still had a trial to face with the threat of a long sentence as a habitual offender. One Sunday Richard attended chapel and heard Peter Cherevchenko, the enormous Russian immigrant, tell how his life had been changed while in jail.

"I went to chapel before that just to be with friends," Richard said. "This time, in spite of his thick accent, I understood every word."

Peter told how his spiritual experience, which started in jail, had followed him to his life outside. It was real. From that day on, Richard believed it could work for him on the outside as well.

Before going to trial, the public defender, Mr. Duffy, told Richard, "Be honest with me, and I'll try to get you as little time as possible. Tell me your story."

"I'm guilty," Richard said.

"What?"

"I'm guilty."

Disconcerted, Mr. Duffy asked, "What do you mean?"

"Well, it was my dope the police found. I thumped it, and they found it." A few weeks before, he would have lied and said anything to get out of jail. Now he surprised himself with his honesty. He didn't try to explain his conversion. He didn't think anyone in court would understand.

Mr. Duffy continued, "Would you say this in court?"

"I'll tell it to anybody."

"Wait a minute; I'll be right back."

Mr. Duffy returned smiling. "This is sounding good. Now you really meant what you said? Don't change on me now."

In the courtroom the judge asked the police for their story and then asked Richard for his. Again he repeated, "I'm guilty. It was my dope they found." Instructing Richard to go back to the bullpen, the judge said they would go into his chambers with the case.

Then Richard was called out, and the judge spoke to him. "Mr. Russell" (he had never been called mister in court before), "we have argued your case in my chambers. It rests. You are free to go."

Immediately Richard lifted his face and said, "Thank you, Jesus." Then he smiled at the judge. "Thank you, Your Honor. Thank you, Mr. Duffy."

Back in the cellblock, the prisoners asked Richard, "What happened?"

"I'm free," he told them.

"Man, you jivin'."

"No, man, I'm free to go."

"Well, why didn't you go on, chump? You in here with us. You ain't free."

In Richard's cell the prayer band gathered, and while they were on their knees, a guard called, "Richard Russell, get your things. Let's go." So on November 16, 1964, Richard Russell, with a new commitment to Jesus Christ

153

just two months old, went forth as inmates gathered around saying, "Hey, can I join the prayer band? Pray for me, man."

Richard had been on probation when he was busted in the summer, but he hadn't been reporting. Once before he had reported when he was high, and they had sent him back to jail. This time he went to the probation office, knowing he was in violation, and asked to have everything set straight. It might mean another sentence, he knew, but he was determined. Leafing through the record, the officers couldn't find his name.

"It's got to be there," Richard insisted. "Just keep looking."

Finally they found it. "Oh, you've been discharged from probation," they told him. Once again he went away thanking God.

Weeks before this, he had written to his mother about the change in his life, and now she let him come home to live. Then his former girlfriend asked him to move in with her, but after a few weeks he realized he'd have to give that up. Studying the Bible, attending church, and praying, he knew it was wrong.

Whenever the church had a meeting, Richard was the first one there. Since he was always waiting on the street for someone to open up, they gave him a key, and he went in to turn on the heat and clean up the church while waiting for others.

He also wanted an honest job, but finding one with his record was difficult. Eventually he started working at a junkyard on Lake Street, but after one month, his boss casually commented, "Boy, Richard, it's cold out here."

Replied Richard, "Not to me." It was snowing and the ground was icy, but Richard didn't mind. He was happy to have a job, any kind of job, thinking, *I am so glad to be doing something right after all those years of doing wrong.*

"Well, it's so slow now," his boss went on. "Come back in the summer, and maybe I can find work for you again."

Dejected, he trudged home slowly through the snow, pulling his thin coat around him. It *was* cold, really cold; he just hadn't noticed it before. He had no money, and the only thing he owned was an old suit that Goodwill Industries had given him. The one thought that came to his mind was that he would have to work at something he knew how to do and something he did well—stealing cars. With a screwdriver, Richard could get into a car, pop the ignition switch out, and drive away within a minute and a half.

Entering his mother's basement apartment, he looked around until he found a screwdriver. Then he sat in the semidarkness, hands in his lap, rolling the yellow plastic handle back and forth. To lull his conscience that kept pricking him, he reasoned, "If I have to steal cars for a while until I can get a job, I'll make it right later. Besides, I never steal from poor people, only from the affluent who have insurance on their cars anyway. I'm not really hurting anyone. The insurance companies have plenty of money, and I have nothing."

With the screwdriver in his coat pocket, he went to church and listened to his brothers and sisters pray and share stories of their Christian life. Then he felt compelled to stand up. He held up the screwdriver and told them about his dilemma. His mother reached out her hand and said, "Son, I'll take that," and he dropped it into her outstretched palm. She put it in her purse while they all prayed for Richard to have the strength to overcome the temptation. And they prayed that God would provide another job for him.

Soon he found a job at Henrici's Restaurant in Chicago's Merchandise Mart, and no one asked about his

155

past or had him fill out an application form that re-
quested that information. Knowing nothing about his
background, they gave him keys and let him open the
restaurant in the morning and close it at night. He was
filled with gratitude that he was now trustworthy, something he had not been since he was a very small child.

At church Richard began to watch Cora, who taught
the young-adult Sunday school class. She was well respected by everyone and responsible; she had worked at
the same job for six years. One time, as the church members formed a car pool to attend a meeting elsewhere, the
pastor assigned Richard and Cora to the same car, and
Richard thought to himself, *Maybe this is my wife.* Several
weeks later the pastor said privately, "Sister Cora, God is
going to give you a husband."

Richard and Cora had never had a date when he con-
fronted her with the message "God told me you were to
be my wife." But Cora believed him, and together they
went to the home of an aged wise woman in the church,
who always wore a white cotton dress. She counseled with
them and asked questions. Five months later, they were
married.

It wasn't until two years after his release that Richard
felt he had to come back to the jail to tell me what had
happened to him. Late one chilly fall morning I left the
building on an errand. As I stepped out to the street, a
black man approached me, grinned, and stretched out
his hand. I didn't recognize Richard.

"You remember me? I accepted the Lord in your office. I've come back to thank you."

I needed that that morning, and as I saw the glow on
his face, I thanked God once again for keeping me there.
We went to a nearby coffee shop. Several weeks later
Richard went with me to a church meeting to tell his
story, and we began to keep in touch.

When the PACE program began, Richard volunteered to follow up some of the released trainees. Who knew better the problems a man faced getting out? For a while we put him on the payroll as a part-time counselor, and then hired him full-time. Today the man who once thought that the worst part of going to jail was getting out is helping men who feel the same way.

About a month before a trainee's release, Richard forms a plan for him. Where will he work? Where will he live? What will keep him from going back to the old life? On the big day, he walks up the long corridor with the inmate to the front desk, helps him with the right papers, then walks with him out the front door.

If the inmate is on probation, their first stop may be the probation office to find out when to report. They establish the habit of doing it right. Then they stop at a currency exchange to cash a check. While enrolled at PACE, the student has received twenty dollars a week through the Comprehensive Employment Training Act. He could spend up to five dollars a week at the jail commissary, but he had to put at least fifteen in an allowance account. Now he has a small nest egg to help to get started outside.

With that cared for, Richard drives the man home to meet his family. He wants to start a good relationship with them as well. The next day Richard's back again, hanging on like a shadow, building the ex-prisoner's confidence, passing on counsel and suggestions, helping him slowly fit into the routine of outside life.

Richard was assigned the case of Danny Morris, a twenty-five-year-old former thief and drug addict with no work record. In six months at PACE, Danny got his first Social Security card and a high-school diploma as well as some practical experience in repairing electrical motors. When he got out, his mother didn't want him, so

157

Richard found him a temporary home at a Salvation Army shelter. Then he drove him to Coyne American, a vocational school, and enrolled him.

In six months he graduated from Coyne with honors and did so well on his job that they made him a supervisor. Richard had pulled back by this time, but he gave Danny a small white card that read "Richard Russell, PACE," and a phone number. "Call me," he told Danny, "any time of day or night if you need me."

Early one morning Danny called Richard from the House of Correction. He had been partying with some friends the night before and had gotten arrested for disturbing the peace. It was Richard's day off, but he picked up Danny's check at work, talked to his boss, who wanted him back on the job, and got him out on bond. Two days later Danny was back at work, repentant, thankful, and determined to find out what made Richard Russell care the way he did.

TO
REPAIR
A BREACH

FIFTEEN

ACCORDING TO COOK COUNTY JAIL officials, three out of every four men they release will return to jail, some of them within weeks. Accurate statistics are difficult to get, but as nearly as we can tell, only one out of every four PACE graduates have returned to jail in the past ten years. That may not be the best way to judge a program, but it does say something.

I tend to look at individual lives rather than numbers, however. When I see a column of statistics, I think of someone such as Mac. He already had a high-school diploma when he came to us and had worked on the railroad for three years. He didn't have any real work skills, however, so he began taking electronics courses at PACE. When he got out, we helped him enroll in electronics school.

Mac is a moody guy, saddled with family problems and a gang of "friends" who would lead him back to jail if he'd let them. When his wife threatened to leave him and he

161

couldn't find a job in electronics, he hit the bottom emotionally. Rather than throw it all over, however, he did what we urge all PACE graduates to do—he called his counselor.

The counselor arranged a job interview with Sears, who were looking for TV repairmen. But Mac, certain he'd be rejected, refused to go. It took some patience and persistence on the counselor's part to get him there, and he got the job. Today he still works for Sears, owns his own truck, and has a route he works exclusively in the homes of people who at one time wouldn't let him past the front door.

Or take Fred, who, after seven months and eight days in Cook County Jail, took a job as a carpenter. Fred had been arrested for stealing to pay for his drug habit. While most of the men in the carpentry program in PACE had started out building shoeboxes, Fred had built a model house with the aid of a Chicago architect who volunteered his time in the evenings. Today he's building real houses.

Both Mac and Fred have more than new skills to rely on, however. For one thing, they have more confidence in their own ability to stay out of jail, and they have a better appreciation for themselves. We can measure increased reading ability, but we can't measure the amount of self-esteem these men have gained. If I want to convince a prisoner of anything, it's that he has a right to succeed.

Again, while staying out of jail may not be the best measure of success, we get a special thrill every time we hear about a graduate who has done well on the outside. One day while working on this book, Dell called the IBM typewriter repairman. When she told the voice on the other end that this was a PACE typewriter, the repairman responded, "You're kidding."

162

"No, I'm not. Who is this?" Dell asked, puzzled.

"This is Mike," came the cheery response. "I'm a PACE graduate. Remember me? I've been working here for months now. Say hello to everyone for me."

Then of course there are the twenty-five percent who come back to Cook County Jail. Willie, my present clerk, is a good example. While he is a recidivist, he's not a failure.

About a year and a half ago, Willie got out of jail. With no place to live or work, we invited him to stay at our house and gave him a job as a purchasing agent for PACE. He managed well for several weeks, but then we saw a quandary building in his life. Being free with a job and a chance at a new life wasn't enough. He started grumbling, wanting a nice car and expensive clothes, things he never had to wait for when he carried a gun. He realized that living a new life meant he would have to change, and he was sure he couldn't.

Scared, he ran. One Saturday he rented a car from an agency two blocks from our house and disappeared for several weeks. Like a young colt, there was so much to run to that he just couldn't cope. It was easier to do wrong, and once he started slipping, he was too ashamed to ask for help. He kept telling himself, "I'd rather be dead than face Pa [his name for me]. If I'm caught, I'll resist and get killed rather than face the man I've failed."

Willie had been born out of wedlock and taken by his grandmother at six weeks. She gave him the name Taylor, which he believed was his real name, until he joined the Marines and saw that his birth certificate showed his name as Carter. Later he was told that his mother had legally changed his name to Morris, his father's name. He never knew if he were Willie Carter, Willie Taylor, or Willie Morris. Not sure who he was or whom he belonged to, blaming his mother, he had

163

headed for the streets, and that led to jail.

Two weeks after he left our house, he was caught stealing a truck, but he couldn't resist as he had planned, and he wasn't freed on bond as his accomplices were. That next night one of them was shot and killed, and Willie might have shared this fate if he had been released with them.

Back in the Cook County Jail receiving room, a guard told Willie that I would be up to see him soon, and he thought, *How am I gonna face him?* He had not cried in years and didn't think he could. When he saw me, his eyes became watery.

"How are you, Willie?"

"Fine."

"Well, Willie, what you've done is part of the past. We have to think about the future. Do you want to work for me again?"

He would have felt better if I had slapped him, he said later. After I left, he wept, his aching spirit broken.

Our kids telephone and visit Willie in jail. Gregg phones often, telling him, "Willie, we're all waiting for you to get out. I love you, Willie." Our children, of course, through guys like Willie, have learned a lot about forgiveness, tolerance, and unconditional love.

Recently Willie asked our family to come and celebrate the commitment of his life to Christ. He said we had never preached to him nor urged him in any way, but he had watched us and learned what the Christian life was all about. "I didn't know there were any for-real people in the world," he told me. "I've been to a lot of churches and known a lot of ministers, but they were all bootleg preachers, out for money." So Dell baked a birthday cake, and we took it to the jail to celebrate. We formed a circle around Willie and asked the Lord to help him live a new kind of life.

When Willie gets out of jail, we hope he will be able to stay out. But whether he does or not, we know God is always working in his life, and stumbling is part of learning to walk. And when we stumble in the Christian life, God reaches out his hand to help us up and steady us as we walk again.

Before we had any money to hire a staff, we found men and women who were willing to give their time to tutor and teach the inmates. They didn't stop coming, however, when we finally got funds. We had more and more inquiries—a call from a church, someone who had heard me speak at a service club, or someone who had heard about PACE through a friend.

When I spoke at a Presbyterian church near Chicago several years ago, the senior art director for a large Chicago agency spoke to me. Obviously moved, he asked if I could use his talents in the jail. While it sounded good to me, I didn't hold my breath waiting. It happens every time I speak; some with tears in their eyes come promising to help, but most never show. Of those who do come, only a handful keep coming back.

Frank Nicholas came the next week. He's been coming once a week now for seven years.

I can't explain the rapport he has with prisoners. He's a straight, no-nonsense kind of guy, very serious. He insists on small classes when he teaches art, and while the students are drawing they talk about a lot of things.

One night a student excitedly told Frank, "I'm readin' the Bible."

"What part are you reading?" Frank asked.

"Man, I'm a-readin' the 'Revolution.' "

Trying not to smile at this mispronunciation of Revelation, Frank wondered what the jail authorities might

165

think if they heard that Mexican inmates were excited about revolution.

Another student, who knew nothing about art but was anxious to learn, was instructed to draw a hand. "It looked more like a gorilla's foot than a human hand," Frank said later. But after two lessons the student had made phenomenal improvement, and Frank's genuine appreciation and praise encouraged him even more.

It isn't always that easy, though. Frank told me recent ly, "Right now, I have a guy in my class who hates me so much I can feel the heat. He's rude, disruptive, and makes fun of me. But really I try to let God's love break through to him. I've seen it happen before."

One night a student asked, "What color is God?"

Frank replied, "I don't really care."

Another time one asked, "How are you gonna rectify what the white man has done to the black man?"

"I can't. There is no way I can bring justice to a situation like that. All I can do is share my life with you."

Inmates are always asking volunteers, "Why are you here? Do you get paid? Are you writing a paper for college?" When a student asks Frank why he's there, he answers honestly. "I want to help." This often leads to more questions about his Christian faith, about God and the Bible, but Frank also does a lot of listening and a lot of encouraging and affirming. Most of the prisoners feel they can't do anything right; they need constant building. Frank's work doesn't end there, however. When a student is released, Frank encourages him to telephone him at work, and often he has former inmates in his home.

"I'm appalled that there are not more Christians involved in PACE," Frank laments.

If a prisoner finds a relationship with Jesus Christ this way, as often happens, it's because of the same principle that worked in my life and in Joel Ayres and in hundreds of others. God becomes real through the life of someone who cares. The gospel takes on human form. Christ lives in the life of a Frank Nicholas, and his students know it's real.

Frank, of course, is only one of about 150 volunteers who come into the jail each week. PACE uses college students, business executives, housewives, retired people (some in their seventies). Bank employees give courses on money management; nurses teach personal hygiene. Most of the volunteers help as tutors with math and reading. Not all the volunteers have the same Christian commitment Frank has, and all of them aren't as well equipped to give spiritual counsel. But God has sent his people, and the demonstration of love in action often counts more than any kind of professional training.

I appeared one noon on "The Lee Phillip Show," a popular TV talk program in Chicago, and received a call from a viewer, a pastor wanting to start "group meetings" in the jail. I had just told Lee Phillip that we needed volunteers, yet I was skeptical of this one.

For one thing, a lot of people have begun new programs at the jail and given up after a few weeks. Nothing hurts us more. I was also cautious when I heard the denomination this man was from.

Eventually, however, the pastor put us in touch with one of his members, Marty Pratt, a salesman for General Mills; he called himself "a glorified Wheaties peddler." I liked Marty, but I had to be careful. He came to the jail, and it seemed to me that his warm, caring way must be an evidence of the Holy Spirit in his life. Still, I put him off for more than six months.

When Marty persisted, I finally let him start a group—under my watchful eye, of course. He brought a friend, Karl Grant, who had only recently committed his life to God. They began sharing groups: Bible study meetings in which prisoners shared personal experiences, problems, and joys, and also prayed, encouraged, and supported one another.

Slowly my doubts faded. Marty and Karl kept coming, driving an hour each way, week after week, and I could see that inmates responded to them. It wasn't the "chaplain" and the "counselee" talking. It was just a group of Christian brothers helping each other as the Bible teaches, and there was an openness and genuineness about the groups that I couldn't miss. I was again reminded that real Christianity existed outside of my own small circle.

In one of the dark days when I wondered if I'd weather the storms that hit our little project, I went to hear a preacher named Ben Johnson.

I was disappointed, however, when he announced he was going to preach on the verse "What shall it profit a man, if he shall gain the whole world, and lose his own soul?" I'd heard that verse, quoted it, and preached on it so many times I was sure he couldn't wring anything new out of it.

I was wrong. Each of us are unrepeatable miracles of God, he pointed out. No one in the past has experienced my dimension of life, nor will anyone in the future. I'm unique. To "lose your own soul," Johnson said, means to lose your authentic self. Not to develop that authentic self would be to deprive the world of one facet of God's glory.

I have a tape recording of that message, and I've listened to it many times as I've thought about my own future. I realize that the *most important thing in my life is to be the person God wants me to be.* God has had a plan, a path

168

just for me, even from the bewildering years of my childhood and up to the present. And his plan stretches on into the future. I've been offered some prestigious, lucrative positions, but I'm convinced for now that my authentic self and ministry are to be found in Cook County Jail. I have promised God and myself that I will never leave this place until I have as direct a call to leave as I did to come.

I'm trying to learn to be who I'm meant to be, and this is a lot more fun, with much less pressure. It takes away jealousies and resentments of other people's accomplishments. Our gifts, regardless of how insignificant they may appear to us, are of utmost importance to God.

I have dreams for PACE, and I'm trying to learn whether or not they're God's dreams. I'd like to build a center for former inmates where they can continue their education and get their feet on the ground. We'd provide counseling services, recreation, temporary living quarters.

We already have the property—four acres of land on the West Side of Chicago that Richard Ogilvie was instrumental in having donated to us. It's beginning to look as though this dream will come true.

Now the county has asked us to design an educational program for the entire Cook County Department of Corrections, to include some four to five thousand people. We have a task force looking at the idea. My main concern is that in growing we don't lose what's vital. It's the people in PACE who have made it what it is. It's that retired carpenter who travels an hour each way by bus and train one evening a week, or the young lady from a nearby college who patiently rehearses prisoners in their multiplication tables and nurses them from illiteracy to an adult reading level. These people give something to the prisoners at Cook County Jail that no educational plan or paper can describe.

Not long ago I drove down through central Indiana with my wife and children, visiting the foster homes, the boarding houses, and the institutions of my youth. Slowly I began to uncover some of the past that I had carefully buried, that I had pushed out of my mind because it was too painful to carry around. As we rolled across the Indiana countryside, I saw a picture of myself time and time again sliding down a precipice, but each time God provided a branch for me to cling to. I could look back and see his hand in my life, and I could trace the path of one event after another leading me to where I am today.

At the same time, I thought about my sisters, both of whom are still struggling as adults. Both have spent the years looking for love. They each have had three children, and in all of them I can see the scars of their mothers' childhoods repeated. Louise now appears to have a stable marriage, but Joan continues to battle with alcoholism.

Such tragedy reinforces in my mind the need for my work and ministry. God salvaged my life so I could reach out to help salvage others. I want to help heal the hurts in the lives of the men and women God sends my way, give them what others have given me, and set them on the same road of self-understanding and right relationship with God.

The roadblocks and difficulties in the early days of founding PACE simply had to be overcome; after all, human lives were depending on it. The roadblocks and difficulties in the early days of founding PACE simply had to be overcome; after all, human lives were depending on it. During the various storms, I could not discern

170

God's presence, but when the clouds lifted and the skies cleared, I could look back on a long road and see his footprints all along the way.

Whatever lies ahead, I ask only one thing: that God go with me. With his help, I can come to the end of my life and merit an epitaph from the words of Isaiah 58:12, "And thou shalt be called, The repairer of the breach, The restorer of paths to dwell in."

APPENDIXES

HOW TO HELP

If you have been moved to help people in trouble, we hope you will get involved. It is impressive to realize that over four hundred Scripture verses refer to God's concern for the poor and the oppressed.

Some suggestions for working with the incarcerated may be helpful.

People sometimes go to prisoners with extremely harmful attitudes. Some are judgmental; they see inmates as sinners to preach to, who need the gospel more than others. Actually the basic difference between the imprisoned and the free is that prisoners have sinned differently or just happened to get caught.

A common denominator among inmates is the feeling that nobody cares about them and that they are worthless. They need a demonstration of love, not a pronouncement of condemnation. They need understanding people willing to hear inner hurts—people who will realize that environments and circumstances have caused problems to develop. Instead of bombarding inmates with endless verses of Scripture and answers without knowing questions, you need to allow inmates to express themselves. They need to know there is more to religion than just preaching.

Occasionally people are offended when inmates ask for favors instead of spiritual help. Try to realize that most are so emotionally drained that this may be the only way they can respond. Jesus was not upset when people came to him for physical needs. He fed; he clothed; he healed; he listened. These are all ways of opening up lines for deeper communication.

It is also important to go to institutions trying to understand the problems of the administration without being critical of inconveniences and difficulties.

Upon release, inmates need to be forgiven and accepted back into society and into our churches, where they can be nurtured.

Some ways you might help are:
- Writing letters
- Visiting
- Tutoring
- Counseling
- Forming dialogue groups
- Providing literature (correspondence courses, Bibles, etc.)
- Post-release (providing jobs or an understanding ear)

Further information can be obtained from:

PACE INSTITUTE, INC.
Cook County Department of Corrections
2600 S. California Ave.
Chicago, IL 60608
Telephone 312-927-3840

174

AMERICAN CORRECTIONAL ASSOCIATION
L-208 Hartwick Office Building
4321 Hartwick Rd.
College Park, MD 20740

> Covers the spectrum of professions in corrections and publishes a directory of state and federal correctional institutions.

AMERICAN PROTESTANT CORRECTIONAL
  CHAPLAINS' ASSOCIATION
% Rev. Adlai Lucas
South Carolina Department of Corrections
P. O. Box 11159
Columbia, SC 29211

> Lists active Protestant clergy serving in corrections.

AMERICAN CATHOLIC CORRECTIONAL
  CHAPLAINS' ASSOCIATION
% Chaplain O'Brien
P. O. Box 32
Huntsville, TX 77340

> Lists active Catholic clergy serving in corrections.

CHICAGO LAW ENFORCEMENT STUDY GROUP
109 N. Dearborn St.
Suite 303
Chicago, IL 60602

> Publishes a report of criminal justice programs operated by citizens.

GOOD NEWS MISSION
1036 S. Highland St.
Arlington, VA 22204

Provides Bible correspondence courses and chaplaincy services in several states. Has listings of penal organizations.

INTERNATIONAL HALFWAY HOUSE ASSOCIATION
% American Correctional Association
L-208 Hartwick Office Building
4321 Hartwick Rd.
College Park, MD 20740

Publishes directory of halfway houses in United States.

JOB THERAPY, INC.
205 Smith Tower Building
Seattle, WA 98104

An employment agency for both juvenile and adult ex-offenders.

JUVENILE INSTITUTIONS

Under the jurisdiction of local county courts. Contact can usually be made through a pastor.

LOCAL JAILS

Jails are found in most counties and cities throughout the United States and are under the jurisdiction of the local sheriff's office or local mayor. Contact can usually be made through a pastor, local council of churches, or the local ministerial association.

MAN TO MAN PROGRAM
1125 Smith Tower Building
Seattle, WA 98104

Links volunteers with inmates for visitation.

NATIONAL COUNCIL ON CRIME AND
  DELINQUENCY
411 Hackensack Ave.
Hackensack, NJ 07601

> A citizen organization seeking to stimulate community programs for prevention, treatment, and control of delinquency and crime.

SALVATION ARMY
Listed in telephone directory

> Provides services to penal institutions in most areas.

VOLUNTEERS IN PROBATION
200 Washington Square Plaza
Royal Oak, MI 48067

> Helps young people in trouble. Can provide information on how to organize a volunteer program in your area or how to work with an existing one.

ACKNOWLEDGMENTS

Any work that bears a single name should have hundreds written across it. We are dependent upon each other, and God works primarily through people.

PACE has been a unique blending of government, private citizens, religious groups, and the business community, illustrating the fact that crime is everyone's business. In addition to the people and organizations mentioned in this book, I thank the following who have had such an important part in my life.

Personal friends who have been especially supportive:
Christ Church of Oak Brook
Rev. Arthur DeKruyter
Eunice Dressel
Hal and Betsy Edwards
Johnny and Joni Genarella
Dean and Lois Griffith
Neal and Carol Phillips
River Forest Bible Chapel (my ordaining church)
Rev. George Rice
Evelyn and Ernest Sandeen

Special friends of PACE:

PACE staff and board, without whose dedication there would be no program

Chicagoland news media

Safer Foundation

Samuel C. Bernstein, assistant to the mayor for manpower

Michael A. Bilandic, mayor of Chicago

Bernard Carey, state's attorney, Cook County

Dorothy G. Drish, board member, Cook County Department of Corrections

George W. Dunne, president, Cook County Board of Commissioners

Richard J. Elrod, sheriff, Cook County

Emma and Oscar Getz, chairman of the board, Barton Brands

Emanuel Hurwitz, associate professor, University of Illinois

Ray A. Kroc, senior chairman and founder, McDonald's Corporation

Elizabeth and John W. Leslie, honorary chairman of the board, Signode Corporation

Julius Menacker, professor, University of Illinois

Joseph P. Monaghen, manpower services coordinator, Cook County

Phyllis K. Snyder, executive director, Chicago's Alcoholic Treatment Center

Kenneth Taylor, Tyndale House

James R. Thompson, governor of Illinois

Ward Weldon, assistant dean, University of Illinois

Acknowledgments

United States Congressmen from Illinois:

John B. Anderson	Robert McClory
Cardiss Collins	Ralph H. Metcalfe
Edward J. Derwinski	Abner J. Mikva
John N. Erlenborn	Dan Rostenkowski
Henry J. Hyde	Paul Simon

Cook County Department of Corrections:
Phillip T. Hardiman, executive director
My fellow chaplains
Entire staff—particularly Officers LeRoy Gay and Elmer
    Jones, who admit me each day, and Officers Clyde
    Holly and Charles Langdon, who release me each
    evening, with constant cheerfulness and kindness.
    And Sgt. Tom Panish, who keeps all our trainees on
    the correct cellblocks.

Government agencies aiding in program design and fundings:
Office of Manpower, Cook County Board of Commis-
    sioners
Office of Manpower, City of Chicago
Illinois Office of Education—Adult and Continuing
    Education Section, Adult Vocational and Technical
    Education Section
U. S. Department of Labor and regional offices
U. S. Office of Education and regional offices
Illinois State Employment Service
Illinois Law Enforcement Commission
Chicago—Cook County Criminal Justice Commission
Board of Directors, Cook County Department of Correc-
    tions
Chicago Board of Education
Circuit Court of Cook County, Criminal Division
Public Defenders' Office of Cook County

181

Finally, we thank our beloved inmates in the Cook County Department of Corrections, who have greatly enriched our lives, teaching us much about God and his love.

Whatever we have built of value has been done by all of us and many whose names, because of space, cannot be mentioned.